Teaching from the Heart

Reflections, Encouragement, and Inspiration

Sharon M. Draper

HEINEMANN
Portsmouth, NH

Heinemann
361 Hanover Street
Portsmouth, NH 03801–3912
www.heinemann.com

Offices and agents throughout the world

Library of Congress Cataloging-in-Publication Data
Draper, Sharon M. (Sharon Mills)
    Teaching from the heart : reflections, encouragement, and
inspiration / Sharon M. Draper
        p.   cm.
    ISBN 0-325-00131-6 (alk. paper)
    1. Teachers—United States. 2. Teaching—United States.
3. Draper, Sharon M. (Sharon Mills). 4. Teachers—United States
Biography.   I. Title.
LB1775.2.D72   2000
371.1'00973—dc21   99-39534
                                                         CIP

Editor: Lois Bridges
Production: Melissa L. Inglis
Manufacturing: Louise Richardson
Cover design: Barbara Werden Design

Printed in the United States of America on acid-free paper
03   02   01   00   99   DA   1   2   3   4   5

To my parents, Vick and Catherine Mills—
who were my first and best teachers

To my children, Wendy, Damon, Cory, and Crystal—
who taught me more than I taught them

To my husband, Larry—
who has always been my Teacher of the Year

To all of my former teachers—
those I will never forget, and those I cannot remember—
Thank you

To all of my former students—
I remember you all and I love you all—
Thank you

Contents

Contents

Contents

Introduction

I'm a teacher. That is what I am. That is what I do. That's
my passion, my challenge, and my joy. As I approach retirement from one phase of teaching and move to another, I would like to share some of what I learned with
other teachers. Whether you are a student in a school of education, just trying to decide if this is the right place for you,
or a student teacher, or an experienced teacher who is "not
quite burned out, but crispy around the edges," this book is
designed for your inspiration and encouragement.

Teaching is an avocation, not a job, and we who teach
sometimes need to be reminded of the importance of the
work we do. We need to remember the joys, and we need
to listen to someone who understands the difficulties of our
daily activities. We need to be reminded of the faces of the
children who need us. We need to have something to make
us smile at the end of a long day.

Teaching from the Heart is not a reference book or
study guide; it is a book of gems to hold on to when your
world as a teacher seems to be filled with nothing but rocks.

Each chapter is short and easily readable during a hurried lunch hour or during a study hall.

It is also a book that the general public can read and enjoy. Everyone has a commonality in their shared school experiences. Everyone can remember a teacher who shaped or influenced them in some way. To assume that the general public would have no interest in a book about teachers is to assume that the public would have no interest in a book about doctors. Teachers are a part of the fabric of our society, and this book can help remind the public how hard we as teachers work and how much we need to be shown respect and appreciation.

The touch of a teacher on the life of a child truly does make a difference.

First Days

My First Day of School; as a Student Teacher; as a Teacher

I fell out of the car on the way to school on my first day of kindergarten. My mother was driving, and I was sitting anxiously next to her, dressed in a new red plaid dress with red ribbons in my hair. I had waited for school all my life, and five years was a very long time to wait. I dreamed of books and yellow pencils and alphabet letters dancing in a line. I had already spent two years in nursery school, so I could count up to one hundred and knew my ABC's quite well. But this was real school, which promised answers to questions I hadn't even imagined yet.

I leaned very close to the car door, straining to see everything, hoping to remember every moment of that day, when suddenly I leaned too hard on the door handle, the door flew open, and I was tossed onto the middle of the road. These were the days before seat belts were required in cars, when a mother's hand in front of your chest was the only safety device in the front seat, but even my mother's quick reflexes weren't fast enough to catch me. She stopped the car instantly, and ran frantically to where I sat, a little stunned, but unhurt except for a skinned and bloody knee. I cried, not because I was hurt, but because I knew this would make me late for the first day of school.

After proper bandaging and much checking of the rest of my body for injuries, my mother and I set off for school once more. I was subdued and a little angry. I believed I had missed all of the important stuff that my older friends had told me about—the welcome from the teacher, the sitting in the little wooden chairs, the smell of the new crayons. We arrived, my mother took me to the classroom, and after explaining to the teacher what had happened, she gave me a hug and said good-bye. I think she was trying not to cry. I looked around at the sea of strange, curious faces, already seated in the little wooden chairs, just as I feared, and my heart sank. But suddenly one little boy noticed the thick white bandage on my knee. It was very serious-looking, although the wound really didn't hurt much.

"How'd you get that?" he blurted out.

"I fell out of my car," I answered shyly.

"You did? Wow!" he replied with admiration.

"Was the car going fast?" one girl wanted to know.

"Did you get run over?" another asked.

"Was there blood?" a boy inquired.

I was a sudden and instant celebrity. After all, nobody else had come to kindergarten with a fresh white bandage and a wonderful story to go with it. The teacher let the discussion continue for a bit, then showed me a little wooden chair that had been saved just for me.

"I'm not too late?" I asked timidly.

"You're just in time," she assured me, "to help me pass out the crayons." I grinned with pleasure as I inhaled the wonderful smell of crayons on a September day. I limped just a little, to impress the rest of the class, as I proudly passed out the crayons. School had finally begun. I knew I was going to like this place.

A short fifteen years later, I was ready to start my student teaching. I had known that I wanted to teach ever since that first day of kindergarten. I taught my dolls, my cats, and the children next door. The teachers that I encountered were strong and positive and reassuring. I excelled in learning, making honor roll every time and loving every moment of it. I was an avid reader, sometimes reading one hundred books during a summer vacation, digesting information to be used at some later date. I sailed through high school, rolled through college, and waited anxiously to begin student teaching. I had taken all the methods classes and philosophy classes offered, and I knew I was ready to become an effective teacher. In addition, I had already had several jobs in college—as a teacher assistant in various local junior high schools—so I felt comfortable and ready.

It was a dark and rainy morning that first day of student teaching. No bright sunshine to welcome me to teaching, just storm clouds and a chilly rain. I ignored it as I got dressed. I had planned my outfit carefully. I wanted to look professional, and not like a college student. I put on a gray paisley dress with brand new gray shoes. They had large buckles, high heels, and were the height of fashion. I glanced at myself in the mirror, checked my hair and my makeup, and approved. I felt like an adult for the first time.

I arrived at the school in plenty of time, a large sprawling building with what seemed like miles of cement walkways for students and steep granite steps to the huge front doors. I grabbed my briefcase, opened my umbrella, and marched confidently up the cement path to the front steps. But those slippery-soled new shoes and the rain-slicked pavement were not a very good match, and just before I reached the front steps, I fell sprawling in front of the school. My right knee, the same one I had skinned on the first day of kindergarten, was bloody and throbbing, my new pantyhose was ripped to shreds, and my confidence lay tossed with my shiny new empty briefcase.

A security guard hurried to help me and escorted me to the nurse's office, which was not far away. I was embarrassed and angry, and really upset that I would be late to meet with my mentor teacher, who I knew was checking her watch as first bell began and I had not arrived. Once again, even though I tried not to, I cried on the first day of school.

The nurse, a kindly and sympathetic woman, patted my arm and tried to soothe me.

"It's not that bad, dear," she assured me. "I'll just put a bandage on your knee and you can get to class. Who is your teacher? I'll write you a note."

I cried real tears now. "I AM the teacher," I sobbed.

I eventually found my way to class and gave a hurried explanation to my mentor teacher. "I'm not too late?" I asked anxiously.

"You're just in time," she assured me, "to introduce yourself to the class."

I faced a class of quiet and curious ninth graders. Of course the first thing they noticed was not my new paisley dress, or even my badly scraped new shoes, but, of course, that huge white bandage on my right knee. I introduced myself to them, but before I could do anything else, the questions, which sounded vaguely familiar, began.

"What happened to you ?" one large boy blurted out.

"I fell out of an airplane." I answered with a grin.

"You did? Wow!" he replied with admiration.

"How'd you do that?" a girl asked.

"Skydiving," I replied, not skipping a beat.

"Cool," she said, impressed.

"Was there blood?" a boy inquired. There's always a kid who wants to know about the blood.

Just as in kindergarten, I was a sudden and instant celebrity. After all, nobody else had come to class on that first day of school with a fresh white bandage and a wonderful story to go with it.

"What is skydiving like?" another asked.

"And what does it feel like when you fall?"

They were interested, intent, and I had lied myself into a corner. But all those years of reading and preparation had paid off. I had read novels about skydivers and airplanes and war heroes. I used them all, weaving a tale of suspense and excitement. They sat spellbound. And I survived my first class.

The bell rang, and I grinned with pleasure as I inhaled the wonderful smell of the first day of school on a September day. School had finally begun. I knew I was going to like this place.

One year later, once again it was time to begin a first day of school, the first of many such days. But this time I had been hired as a teacher, with a contract and a paycheck. I approached the first day with anticipation and awe. No shiny high heels this time—just comfortable, well-worn walking shoes. I wore slacks and a jacket instead of a dress, and I put my seat belt on as I drove to the school. I made it there, up the steps, and to the main office all in one piece. I breathed a sigh of relief. *No bandages this time*, I thought triumphantly.

I walked over to the mailboxes and found my name typed neatly on a tiny little cubby. I touched it with exultation and pride and reached inside. Class list sheets, enrollment forms, medical forms—all of the paperwork of the first day. I looked at it with excitement. The only thing I could not find was my classroom assignment. At the very bottom of the stack was a small, handwritten note. It said, "CLASSROOM—ANNEX B-1."

Puzzled, I asked the secretary, the person who runs all schools, what that meant.

"Oh, didn't they tell you, honey? You're going to be bussed with the seventh graders to the annex building, which is that big church down the street. It's just you and four hundred seventh graders in one big room. Have fun!"

I was stunned. I found my way to the busses, loaded up with a crew of noisy and confused twelve-year olds, and was dumped unceremoniously with them in front of an ancient church building. Once inside, we found it was not much different from the secretary's description. No walls, no dividers, just tables, chairs, and miles and miles of kids. The other teachers, who had had sense enough to drive, showed me where section B-1 was, and the kids trooped in. All was chaos and confusion for at least an hour as we shouted and tried to match children to chairs. I had thirty-five students assigned to me. They looked at me with disinterest. The day had been confusing and distracting. They pushed and shoved each other and ignored my requests to be quiet. Silence was all but impossible as other teachers in the room, even though they were experienced, tried futilely to get anything done.

Lunch was shipped in. Mountains of boxed lunches to be distributed and then cleaned up. The room after lunch smelled like old lunchmeat and orange peels. Where was that refreshing smell of new crayons or waxed hallways of the past? This was not what I had imagined when I had anxiously anticipated my first day of teaching. The day moved as slowly as the thick heat in that windowless room. The students were irritable, the other teachers were just as uncomfortable, and no instruction was taking place. I walked behind the last table, trying to get the attention of a girl who had given up and gone to sleep. Just as I reached her, my soft, comfortable walking shoes connected with an orange peel, and I slipped and went sprawling onto the floor.

Needless to say, she woke up. I was unhurt, except for my pride, as the entire room of four hundred sweating seventh graders rolled in laughter. Instead of being angry or upset, I joined them. I laughed until tears ran down my face. As we laughed together, a bond was formed. In spite of the difficulties, we would make it through this. A couple of the boys helped me up, one of the girls offered to comb my hair, and all of them looked at me a little differently.

I grinned with pleasure as I inhaled the wonderful feel of the first day of school on a September day. School had finally begun. I knew I was going to like this place.

Dear Friend

A Letter to Prospective Teachers

Dear Friend,

Who would ever want to be a teacher? A teacher makes no money, gets no respect, and makes no difference to anyone! Now wait a minute. Is this true? Or are we listening to exaggerations and remembering stereotypical images of the bespectacled, mean Miss Crabtree from old movies? Think back to all of the teachers that you have encountered in your years of schooling. Which one stands out in your memory? What grade?

- The kindergarten teacher who was not afraid to give a hug when needed?
- The third-grade teacher who taught you the magic of cursive writing?
- That fifth-grade teacher who took your class on field trips to museums and concerts?
- The history teacher who showed you the world of humanity?

- The math teacher who taught you not only the intricacies of numbers but also the practicalities of balancing a checkbook and figuring the discount at a sale?
- The science teacher who showed you how the physical and the natural world worked together to give us life on earth?
- The gym teacher who showed you how good it felt to run fast and push yourself to the limit?
- The music teacher who showed you that a complete individual needed a full complement of expression?

Somewhere in your educational career, one or more of these outstanding individuals opened your mind and showed you the way. That teacher made a difference in your life.

And if you become the parents of the twenty-first century, with young ones to care for and educate, who will teach those children? Who will make a difference in the lives of the next generation? If none of you choose to go into education, to make a positive difference on the lives of children who are not even born yet, who will be there to guide them, or direct their minds through the beauty and complexity of the vast wealth of knowledge that we now control?

As you consider teaching as a career, I'd like to offer my own personal response to teaching as a profession. My students often ask me, "Why are you a teacher?" implying that teaching is a terrible career choice. I tell them in response, "I teach because I need you as much as you need me. I teach because once upon a time a teacher made a difference in my life, so I am here to make a difference for you." I was probably born to be a teacher. I never wavered in my desires and determination to become not just a teacher but a really good teacher who made memories in the minds of children. From my early days of student teaching, when I learned that acting out history made it memorable for me as well as my students; to my first teaching assignment, where I broke down and cried in front of the class because thirty-five disruptive students in a makeshift, renovated classroom did not fit my glossy vision of educational excellence; to today, where my seniors wear T-shirts proudly proclaiming, "I survived the Draper Paper," I continued to try to make a difference—one child at a time. For our greatest accomplishments in education are not the plaques and awards but the smiles and hugs and memories of children touched today and somehow influenced tomorrow.

They ask me about the lack of respect for the profession. I respond with, "Raise your hand if you don't respect me!" They grin and see my point. The want to know about the lack of financial rewards. I tell them honestly, "I'll never make what a basketball player makes, but then, neither will most of you. It's not fair that our society pays its entertainers more than its educators, but I make a good living, enough to support a family and send my children to college. And I get extra benefits—smiles, hugs, and the knowledge that what I do really matters."

I once asked a class of fourth graders to give me their definition of a good teacher. These are their responses:

- A good teacher is soft enough to hug, but too hard to punch.
- A good teacher knows lots of dirty jokes but only tells the clean ones that make you laugh.
- A good teacher is not scared of thunder and lightning and knows what to do when the lights go out.
- A good teacher never makes fun of you when you do dumb stuff like throw up or forget the answer.
- A good teacher would be fun to have at your house for dinner, but you'd never want him to come for real.

- A good teacher knows a little bit about a lot of stuff, and a whole lot about things you need to know.
- A good teacher makes you have so much fun you don't know you're learning, and then when you've learned it, you realize it wasn't hard at all.
- A good teacher never has bad breath.
- A good teacher loves you and you know it.

If we could all live up to this simple list, we'd be successful teachers. The children are waiting. Every year, the school year begins a cycle—of freshness and possibility. New shoes, notebooks, and hopes all shine with the beginning of a new school year. As students you accomplished this cycle many times. Each new school year is filled with new hopes and possibilities—new bookbags and textbooks, fresh clean paper, and more often than not, a new teacher to encounter. A teacher who has the potential, just like a new textbook, to open their minds to ideas as yet unimagined. Why not be that teacher? The one who sings the song that you'll always remember. The one who lights the candle that you'll always carry. Are you a potential teacher?

The potential teacher (and practicing teacher as well) should be able to:

- Think positively and enthusiastically about people and their potential. (*Translation:* Tell Frankie, who just threw up on your new shoes, that you really don't care and that you love him anyway.)
- See the good in any situation. (*Translation:* There is gum in your door lock and you have thirty kids sitting in the hall waiting for the janitor, who has had to unstick fourteen locks that morning, so you take them on an in-school field trip and you write down observations of the school at work—the offices, the store-

rooms, the book room, etc. Your kids learn, even in the hallways.)

- Be able communicate effectively. (*Translation:* At the first parents' night you realize that most of the parents of your ESL students speak no English at all, yet you charm them all with your wit and the notebooks their children have done.)

- Be dependable, honest, and consistent. (*Translation:* You will be elected every time to be the faculty fund collector whenever anyone is sick or needs flowers sent or it's time for the annual blood drive.)

- Enjoy personal interaction with others. (*Translation:* You can eat lunch with three hundred hot and sweaty eighth graders and still digest properly even though you only have twenty-two minutes.)

- Be organized and make efficient use of time. (*Translation:* You can put on makeup in the car, grade papers at the dentist's office and at church, and teach five different preparations to seven classes in six different classrooms.)

- Be self-confident, poised, and personally in control of situations. (*Translation:* When you oversleep, dress in a hurry, and are told by your first-bell class that you are wearing one blue shoe and one brown shoe and that your sweater is on backward, you tell them you are beginning a lesson on observation and description and you are proud of their wonderful skills.)

- Have a healthy self-image. (*Translation:* You videotape yourself as you teach and you do NOT think you're too fat, or too thin, or too loud, or too terrible to be a teacher. You see a person with possibilities.)

- Understand how to motivate others. (*Translation:* When Tonya refuses to participate in class and angrily responds to your questions, instead of putting her out of class you talk to her in private. You find out that she can't see the board and her parents can't afford new glasses. You find a fund that provides glasses for kids and she becomes your best instead of your worst student.)

- Have a sense of humor. (*Translation:* When the fourth graders put a snake inside the piano and you open it up to begin class, instead of screaming, you laugh and toss it gently out the window. [You won't die and they'll never do it again.])

Young teachers are waiting, unidentified and unknown, in third-grade and seventh-grade and eleventh-grade classrooms. We must look to students long before they graduate from high school and steer them to a career in teaching. Those students who would be natural teachers are sometimes never identified because no one takes the time to nurture the idea in their minds.

I once had a student named Pedro who was a natural leader of people, an organizer, a lover of knowledge, and a skilled deliverer of information, even at age seventeen. As he approached graduation, I asked him what subject he had chosen as a major. He replied, "I don't know. I'm going to register as 'Undecided.' "

Surprised, I asked him, "Aren't you going to major in education?"

"Why?" he asked. "I never thought about it."

"But you're a natural teacher," I insisted.

"I am?" he asked incredulously.

"Sure," I continued. "You're speak well, learn well, and you know how to share what you know and make someone else understand it. That's a gift. You're a teacher!"

He grinned with recognition of a knowledge that he had not given himself permission to acknowledge. I opened the door to the possibilities, and he is now in his third year as an education major at Ohio State. Suppose no one had had that conversation with him? A wonderful teacher would have been lost.

Think of your parents and what school was like for them. (Very few of them actually walked to school barefoot ten miles every day in deep snow, as they like to exaggerate.) They had no computers, no cell phones, no pagers—none of the modern conveniences that we take for granted. Just as your parents had less to learn than you do, your children will learn more than you can imagine. We need well-trained, dedicated teachers who can make this transfer of vast amounts of knowledge a reality. Children are waiting for a teacher to make a difference in their lives. That teacher can be you.

Help!

I'm Going to Be a Student Teacher!

You started as a student for the first time probably when you were three and first going to preschool. The teacher, someone so much taller than you, but perhaps for the first time, not your mother, loomed at the doorway. The sights and sounds of this new environment looked interesting, perhaps even enticing, but the dominant emotion you felt was fear as your mother left you there to fend for yourself. By the time you got to kindergarten, going to school, and responding as a student, had become familiar and comfortable. For the next twelve or thirteen years you trudged or leaped through school, finally arriving victoriously at high school graduation, only to find that schooling and desks and being a student started once again with a vengeance in college that September. Now, almost twenty years after that first precarious venture into a classroom, it's time to be the teacher instead of the student.

It would seem that student teachers should have it easy. After all, the public reminds us, you've been watching teachers all your life. Doing what they do should be just a matter of repetition and imitation. But teaching is so much more than that. Teaching is a skill that requires practice, dedication, and talent. And time. Time to learn. Time to make mistakes. Time to develop a style.

In most teacher education programs, prospective teachers are given opportunities to observe and interact in classrooms long before student teaching begins. But watching a teacher handle a difficult student and actually doing it successfully is very different. So let's assume you have been given your first student-teaching assignment. What can you do to make it the best opportunity for teaching and learning for you and your students? Finally, you have students. Finally, you are the teacher. Where do you begin?

- Drive by the school. See what it looks like on the outside. What neighborhood is it in? What businesses or homes surround it?
- Go early in the morning as school begins and watch the children enter. Consider the following:
  - Do most of them walk to school (meaning most of them are neighborhood children), or do they arrive on busses (meaning most of them do not live in the neighborhood in which the school is located)?
  - Do many parents drive their children to school?
  - What does the school yard look like? Do the children wait outside before a bell? Are teachers monitoring them? (if so, that will surely be assigned to you at some point)
- Go after school and watch the dismissal routine. Consider the following:
  - Do students leave right away or are numerous children left in the school yard after hours?
  - Do students use the school area as a play space?
  - Are organized after-school activities apparent?

- How soon does the teacher parking area empty of cars?
- Visit the school during school hours. Consider the following:
  - How does the school "feel?" Do the students seem secure and adjusted to school routines? Do the teachers seem relaxed and confident?
  - Locate the cafeteria, library, gym, offices, and rest rooms.
- Talk to your cooperating teacher. Find out his or her expectations as well as fears, and share your own. Set up a time for planning lessons and classroom transition. Find out how much your cooperating teacher will want you to follow his or her lesson plans. Every cooperating teacher is different. Some want you to follow their lesson plans and others encourage you to come up with your own. Find this out early.
- Have you ever written on a chalkboard? Can you write legibly and not make the chalk squeak? Do you know how to use the new white board that many schools now use? What about technology like overheard projectors or projection screens? Make sure you practice these before you try to use them with students.
- In your practicum classes you probably designed lots of lessons and classroom activities and games. Collect those, and put them in a large binder. You never know when one of those will be useful. As you develop more lessons that work, add them to your binder as a record of success as well as specificity.
- Prepare an introductory letter to send parents. In it you want to introduce yourself, ease their fears, and exude confidence. Plan to make direct parental contact for each of your students as soon as possible.

You've completed all the preliminaries. You're ready to begin. You have discarded the book bag for a more professional-looking satchel or case. You've decided against the jeans and the athletic shoes for an outfit that looks professional. For the ladies, your skirts are not too short; for the gentlemen, you have on a sports jacket. Yes, I know all the arguments about civil liberties and personal freedom. But if you wish to present yourself as an adult, ready to take on the world of children, ready to be paid for your services, dress for success. This is the real world.

During the first few days, you will probably just observe, but use this time wisely. Watch everything. From the arrangement of the room to class management techniques, you can learn much about how to handle the class when it is yours. Learn your students' names. You'd be amazed at how effective it can be to address a young person by his or her name. Instead of saying, "You in the third row with the red shirt," you can say, "Robert Thompson, please turn around." The child in the third row might ignore you. Robert Thompson will turn around.

It's finally time for you to take over the class. The mentor teacher is sitting in the back of the room, you are nervous and hesitant, and the students sit waiting, ready to test you. First of all, relax. This is what you've been preparing for all your life. You've prepared, you've planned, and you're ready. Talk to the class honestly. Tell them what your job is and what is expected of them in the process.

Don't be afraid to smile. If it's clear that you like what you're doing, and you know your material, smile and share that with your class. Smiles are infectious. Let the kids know that you like them. Talk to them at lunch, after school, between classes. Find out what they like, what they think, who they really are. Remember, you don't teach a subject—you teach young people.

Have fun! If you present a lesson that seems boring to

you, I guarantee that it will be boring to your students. Let's say you have to teach a lesson on the Civil War. You can have them memorize dates and battles and generals. They will learn very little. Or you can have them research uniforms and living conditions and medical treatment. You can have them act out battles and role-play decisions, participating actively in the fabric of the times. They will never forget it. And neither will you.

Praise them. Young people respond so much better to praise than to criticism. Find something good about even the most difficult students, praise them publicly and honestly, and you will find that they become a little less hard to handle. For example, praise Jerome for getting the first four problems correct instead of berating him for getting the last six problems wrong. He may get the first five right the next time. Let your students have some input whenever you can and let them think they are giving input when you can't. If your goal is to begin a unit on weather, for example, let students offer suggestions about which areas to study. Careful guiding of the discussion will lead them to the areas you had already decided to focus on, and might lead you to new areas as well.

Listen to them. Many of them live in a world that is very unlike the world that many of you are familiar with. That old slogan about walking in other people's shoes begins with listening to the story of the paths they walk upon.

I once spoke to a group of students in an education class. All of them were excited, prepared, and ready for their first teaching assignments. All of them had done well in high school, making good grades and excelling in all things academic. All of them had done equally well in college, some of them making the dean's list while publishing the school newspaper and running track as well. They were well-rounded, intelligent, and ready to teach.

I asked them, "How many of you were really good

students in high school?" All of them quickly raised their hands with pride.

"And how many of you remember those kids in high school who did NOT do well? The kids who skipped classes and talked back to teachers, got suspended from school, and failed several subjects?" They raised their hands, but quizzically, not sure why I was asking them.

"You avoided those kids because they were a bad influence on your academic career, right?" They solemnly agreed.

"When you get your first teaching job," I told them gently, "chances are you will be assigned to teach those very same kids. Do you know how long you have to teach before they let you teach kids like you?" They laughed, but looked concerned. "You will be asked to teach the kids who most need good teachers. Give them your best."

Share with them. When the last bell rings at the end of the day, you'll be tired, drained, and ready to collapse, but don't be in a hurry to rush off. Volunteering with after-school clubs is not only educational for you but it also shows the students another dimension of your personality. They realize that you are really human, and you'll learn the same about them. Stick around for play rehearsal, cheerleader practice, or a baseball game. Kids will remember that you took the time to share your life with them.

Student teaching is an oxymoron. You're a student—still learning—yet you're also a teacher, helping others to learn. It's a time of great frustration and great joy. Preparation will ease the difficulties, and the joy will find you.

A Guide for Student Teachers

An Honest Translation of the Language in Your Assessment Package

What They Say	What That Really Means
Demonstrate proficiency in communication	STUDENT: I don't see why we have to learn no grammar. Don't nobody in my 'hood talk like that. TEACHER: When you're in *your* 'hood, talk any way you like, but when you're in *my* 'hood, we learn to talk the language of jobs.
Use effective teaching components and demonstrate proficiency in their application	STUDENT: Are we doing anything today? TEACHER: We're starting our study of Egypt. STUDENT: We gonna read the chapter and answer the questions in the book? TEACHER: When we get finished with our study of Egypt we will have drawn a map, built a pyramid out of sand, dressed up like a Pharaoh, made up our own hieroglyphics, and learned the riddle of the Sphinx.

Implement successfully a variety of instructional methods and strategies	STUDENT: Do we have to have a spelling test today? TEACHER: Instead of a spelling test today, let's have a spelling bee instead. TEACHER: Instead of a spelling test today, let's write a story today using some of our spelling words. TEACHER: Instead of a spelling test today, let's play spelling bingo.
Analyze and assess students' strengths and needs. Plan and provide appropriate instruction based on individual strengths and needs	TEACHER: Billy, I want you to work with Sara today. She's great with multiplication and you're great with division. The two of you together will be the best math team ever! Here are some flash cards, a computer program, and a game. Have fun!
Balance planning and organization with flexibility and adaptability	TEACHER: OK, class, clear your desks, and let's get ready for this test. We've prepared for this all week. STUDENT: Hey, teacher! There's the fire bell! No test! TEACHER: No problem. We'll review today, have the test tomorrow, and do tomorrow's activities on Monday. Now line up and let's go quietly outside.
Implement effective classroom management techniques	STUDENT: What we gonna do today? TEACHER: Check the board, just like every day. STUDENT: Where do we put our homework?

	TEACHER: In the box on the table, just like we do every day. STUDENT: What should we do first? TEACHER: Write in our journals about the quote of the day, just like we do every day. STUDENT: Lisa keeps jumping up and hogging the discussion. TEACHER: We take turns and listen to each other, just like we do every day. STUDENT: Brad hit me. TEACHER: We keep our hands to ourselves or we stay in for recess, just like we do every day.
Demonstrate interpersonal skills and relations	PARENT: I'm worried about my son Bill. He needs to pass your class to stay eligible for football. TEACHER: I'm concerned about Bill as well. He seems to be torn between sports and music. PARENT: I don't want him wasting his time on music. I want him to get a football scholarship and play for the NFL! TEACHER: Did you know he has a real gift for music? He could get a music scholarship. PARENT: They give scholarships for that? TEACHER: Sure, let's talk to Bill and see if we can keep you both happy and get him successfully into college.

Use questioning techniques that lead students to higher-level thinking and that increase student participation	TEACHER: Why did Goldilocks visit the home of the three bears? TEACHER: What do you think about her visit? TEACHER: What would you think if she had come to your house when you weren't home? TEACHER: What do you think the bears said after she left? TEACHER: How do you think Goldilocks felt when she got home?
Demonstrate adequate knowledge of content	STUDENT: What's wrong with our classroom snake? TEACHER: He's getting ready to shed his skin. STUDENT: How do you know? TEACHER: His eyes are cloudy, and his skin is loose. STUDENT: Maybe he's just going blind. TEACHER: No, he does this about once a month. STUDENT: He looks hungry. TEACHER: He won't eat until he's shed his skin. STUDENT: What can we feed him then? TEACHER: A mouse. He'll eat it whole. STUDENT: Disgusting! TEACHER: I'll let you watch. STUDENT: Cool!

The Story of a School Year

The Cycle of Life

September. (Or maybe late August.) You approach the new year with hope, expectation, and promise. You have new bulletin boards, fresh ideas, and several boxes of tissue. You tell yourself you will be positive, upbeat, and successful with every single child—even Bobby Johnson, who failed sixth grade twice and is now taller than you are.

The kids troop in on that first day, dressed in new everything: new shoes that cost much more than the shoes you wear, new book bags, new blue jeans, long-sleeved wool sweaters. It's ninety degrees outside, but it's new—and by gum, they're going to show it off! They sit there, fresh-faced, hopeful, waiting—waiting for you to unzip their brains and pour in the knowledge. You don't expect them to do anything, do you? Here I am. Pour in it. Don't bother to wake me. Don't try to make me think in the process. Just pour it in. Bobby Johnson sits in the back and says, "I dare you!"

And so the year begins. We dance around each other.

We, the teachers, try to catch the wiggly little minds in a net, while they, slippery little fishes that they are, do everything possible to evade our attempts to capture and educate them.

Leaves fall. The heat finally subsides. Fresh blue jeans start to fade. That Nike swoosh on their shoes and shirts has dimmed to just a comma—which, by the way, is the only place you find them using commas—and the process has begun. Thanksgiving arrives about the time of the first report cards, and some children are thankful that the year has just begun, because grades and learning are still a work in progress. Routines are established by now. When the hall pass can be used. Who collects homework. Who waters the class plants and cleans the hamster cage. The first parent conferences are held. The parents of the kids who most need a conference never show up. When you called Bobby Johnson's parents to invite them to the meeting, they reminded you that they came last year and it didn't do any good. The parents of the kids who make straight A's come early to ask why their child got a B+ on the last assignment. You start to notice patterns of behavior—the students who are always tardy for first bell, the students who are always ill on the day of a test, the students who rarely do homework.

Winter arrives, with snow days and holiday programs and food collections and a short, but welcome, vacation. The heat in the building is often less than needed, just as there is rarely air conditioning on very hot days. You wonder if the business community in the offices downtown would work in such conditions on a daily basis. The class takes up a secret collection to buy you a sweater that is way too small and really ugly, but you wear it with pride. And Bobby Johnson, who still won't do his homework, shovels the walkway to your classroom without being asked.

Are they learning? Have you made the connection? Report cards say some are learning and some need extra help. Tiny victories are often overlooked. A smile. A hug. A thank-you. A "Hey, now I gct it!" or a "Gee, that was fun!" Sometimes it's impossible to see those victories in the gloom of January and February. Soon it's time for proficiency testing. Will they? Can they? Did I? And what about Bobby Johnson?

Spring arrives, slowly this year. Buds appear, hesitant to commit to the weather, which stays cold and dreary. The class moves slowly, as if their brains are clogged with the mud that they bring in on their shoes. Tempers are short, you feel as irritable as they do, and one third of the class is out with a cold. It rains every day for two weeks and your spirits are as damp as the soggy papers they turn in. Bobby Johnson, still as hesitant as a daffodil to let anyone know that he can learn, might not make it out of sixth grade, again.

Finally, slowly, the sun shines on the classroom, no longer pristine and shiny as it was on that first day. It's dusty and cluttered with charts and drawings and artwork. The boxes of tissue have long since been sneezed on and discarded. The crayons, every single one of them, are broken and dumped unceremoniously in a shoe box. The room is full of classwork and homework and successes and failures, and crumpled bags left over from the party held the day the whole class passed the spelling test. It's full of memories. It smells like chalk dust and floor wax and grins and cheers, and tears.

Soon they will leave the classroom as it was on that first day—empty. But it will be forever changed, stained with the shadows of the spirits of that class. It will never be the same, and neither will you. For now that classroom holds the footprints of Tasha, whose mother died in November; and Michael, who underwent cancer surgery in January; and Lena, who finally mastered the mysteries of multiplication in March; and Bobby Johnson, who just barely, but finally, finished sixth grade!

It was a wonderful year. As are they all. For with all of its joys and sorrows, victories and defeats, those footsteps left in the dust of that empty classroom on the last day of school is why we teach. Yes, the floors will be swept, the boards will be washed, the clutter will be removed. And we'll be back again the next fall to do it all again. Why? Because those footsteps will never be swept from our heart. We keep them with us always, the Lenas and the Tashas, and even the Bobby Johnsons. For each year is a wonder and marvelous memory unto itself. So enjoy your few brief moments of summer. Reflect on the past. Prepare for the future. September is approaching. And Bobby Johnson's younger brother will be there waiting for you! He's going to need a hero. He's going to need you.

Advice to a First-Year Teacher

"They're All LOOKING at Me!"

"They're all LOOKING at me!" the new teacher gasped on the first day of class. She smiled, managed to take attendance, and began the activities of the morning. Her face showed confidence; her heart was gripped with fear. Fear that she would make a mistake, not know the right answer, or forget a child's name. Fear that she would never succeed as a teacher. She could not know at that moment that she would make many mistakes, forget many a child's name, and have to learn to admit that she didn't know the answer. She would learn, through that year and the next few years, that mistakes are the best way to learn, that children are extremely flexible and are most cheerfully willing to supply a name or a date or a comma that the teacher misses, and that the best way to teach the art of not knowing is to teach the skill of finding where the correct answer lies.

That new teacher could be anyone. Even though student teaching is a wonderful preparation for the reality, nothing can ever really prepare a new teacher for the enormous responsibility of handling a full-time, full load of classes. The paperwork, the physicality, the mental and emotional preparation are all draining and can be discouraging. Even a well-planned lesson can explode in failure. The ability to adjust and adapt is critical.

A new teacher once showed me her carefully planned vocabulary lesson for a seventh-grade class. The words were on their reading level, covered a variety of word roots and vocabulary skills, and were neatly typed on a worksheet. The lesson was an absolute failure. The students dutifully looked the words up in the glossary and copied the definitions—and the knowledge was transferred from dictionary to ditto sheet without ever having to pass through the brains of the children at all. They remembered none of the words the next day; they barely remembered the activity. After we discussed how she could adjust and make this activity a meaningful learning experience, she tried again. This time, the students generated their own vocabulary list by finding the words from newspaper and magazine articles. They defined the words initially using context clues, then challenged each other to find the correct definitions. Then they made up sentences that used their own names and information from their own lives that used each of the vocabulary words. Not only did the students respond with excitement and enthusiasm, they remembered all of the words the next day, the next week, and the next month. And they begged to do that activity again.

The teacher enjoyed the lesson, as did the students, and learning occurred for both. Learning should be fun and painless, not hard and laborious. If the teacher is enthusiastic and creative, the students will follow.

But suppose I can't do anything fun in my classroom because I can't let them get out of their seats? I'm afraid I'll lose control. Classroom management constantly looms as one of the biggest problems for beginning teachers. How do you make them sit down and pay attention? How do you get them all to be quiet at the same time? It is necessary to establish standards of behavior in order to relax them. Again, if students are allowed to be part of the process of creating the rules of order for the classroom, they are more likely to cooperate in their continuation. Students are like flowers. They need the solidity of the earth to ground them, the warmth of the sun to encourage them, the coolness of the rain to nurture them, and an occasional storm to remind them of the power of the natural rules of order in which they live. Young teachers must find the gentle balance between earth and sun and rain for their students and realize that storms can be very destructive.

That takes practice. It takes experience. And it takes time. Reading about educational psychology will never prepare a young teacher for the realities of classroom behavior. They have to live it. A young teacher once asked me, with great embarrassment, if she could discuss a problem she was having in her class.

"I have a student who has very disturbing behavior," she began. "And I don't know how to handle it."

"What is the problem?" I asked. She was reluctant to tell me.

"He barks," she said finally.

"What have you done to modify his behavior?" I asked her.

"I read every single book I could find on juvenile behavior and abnormal adolescent psychology," she anguished, "but not one of them has a chapter on what to do if a student barks. I've called his parents and the counselor. Nothing helps. He's still barking. What should I do?"

"Bark back," I said simply.

She looked at me incredulously, but followed my advice, and admitted with a smile of relief the next day that the problem had been solved. When the boy asked to go to the bathroom, she barked her response to him. When he asked how to do the homework, she barked the answer. One day was enough. He gave in with a grin.

Of course, that tactic could have backfired. She could have ended up with a class full of barking children. But she had established a standard of classroom behavior based on order and camaraderie. The other students, instead of siding with the disruptive student, saw that it was to their advantage to stay silent and let the teacher handle the problem. Since she did it with grace and a smile, the entire class, including the barking boy, grew closer instead of more distant.

I remember one such disruptive student who purposefully tried to challenge me. He loved basketball and played at lunch every day. My class, which was right after lunch, was an unwelcome interruption to his ball playing. So he came in every day, angry, sweaty, and bouncing his basketball.

The bell rang. *Bounce. Bounce. Bounce.*

The class took their seats and he took his. *Bounce. Bounce. Bounce.*

He watched to see if I was becoming annoyed. *Bounce. Bounce. Bounce.*

"Let's put the ball away now, Rocky." *Bounce. Bounce. Bounce.*

"I think that's enough now. Put the ball away." *Bounce. Bounce. Bounce.*

The class got quiet. They watched with silent excitement the battle of the dueling wills of Rocky and me. *Bounce. Bounce. Bounce.*

I had several choices. I could snatch the ball away. But Rocky was much bigger than I, and he had something to prove. I could scream and yell. I could send him out to the principal's office. Or I could be creative, and turn a losing situation for both of us into a win. *Bounce. Bounce. Bounce.*

"I tell you what, Rocky," I began. "You put the ball away now, and I will *challenge* you to a game of one-on-one tomorrow on the courts at lunch. Bring your friends, unless you don't want them to see you lose." *Bounce. Boun . . .* He dropped the ball and looked at me with a face of incredulity.

"You challenging *me?*" he said in amazement. "There's no way you can beat me!"

The class relaxed. The bouncing had stopped. I had won, for the moment.

"Yeah, I'm challenging you," I countered. "Don't you know I used to play professional basketball? I once played Kareem Abdul-Jabbar and beat him!"

Of course, none of this was true, but he didn't know that. He put his ball away, got out his books, and chuckled at the foolish old teacher who had the nerve to think she could beat him.

The next day at lunch, Rocky and twenty or thirty of his closest friends waited for me on the basketball court. I showed up, bouncing a bright pink basketball with *Barbie* written on the side. They hooted with laughter. I took a shot. I missed. He took a shot. The ball zipped into the basket like silk. He beat me 99 to nothing. That's what I had intended. The kids laughed, cheered me for being a good sport, and Rocky was a hero at my expense.

When class began after lunch, Rocky was laughing and pleasant. All of the students, of course, had heard of my humiliation on the courts. Rocky, to his credit, didn't boast. He didn't need to. He never bounced his ball in class again. And he became a grudgingly cooperative student, willing to make the effort for what I asked of him in class because I had been willing to make an effort for him.

If you want to expand the world of your students, it's wise to find out what that world is, and what place they hold in their world. Only then can you lead them to the world of learning and opportunity.

Candles

*Light Your Candles and
Let Them Shine*

Each of us who are educators have been given one bright and shining star to hold in our hand. It shines like a candle on a table. It glows with hope and possibility. Visualize a glowing candle. The tiny points of light at its edges pierce the darkness. The center glows with golden intensity. That light is knowledge. It is learning. It is the essence of education. That light is the children in our classrooms.

That light is Keisha. She was fourteen. She was brilliant. She used to tell me, "Miss Draper, I'm gonna be a doctor. I'm not going to be like my sister and my cousin and the other girls in my neighborhood—I'm gonna be a doctor!" On the last day of school she came to tell me she was pregnant. I asked what she was going to do, and if she planned to follow her dream of becoming a doctor. She said, "I understand reality. No matter what you say, I'll never be a doctor now. But you know what? My baby's gonna be a doctor—best one you ever saw!"

That light is Q. He had green hair, black fingernails,

and safety pins in his lips and ears. Sometimes he'd spike his hair so it stood straight up. He sang in a group called the "Metallic Chicken People." And he made straight A's. He always said "yes, ma'am" when he spoke to me, and I never heard him say a negative word about anybody. I asked him once why he dressed like that. He responded simply, "Because I can." He said, "I'm sixteen years old and I'm doomed to be a corporate lawyer like my dad. I'll get rid of this look eventually. In the meantime, want to come ride the bus with me? I sit next to little old ladies and growl. Freaks 'em out every time!" I saw Q. not long ago in the mall. I hardly recognized him. He had on a three-piece suit and just a tiny earring in one ear. He hugged me, told me he was a public defender and worked cases against his dad. He loved it. For old times' sake, he growled just once more.

That light is Rick Johnson. He doesn't look much like a star or a candle or any kind of light. He's hungry, and angry, and abused. I wrote a poem about Rick, and kids like him. It's called "Band-Aids and Five-Dollar Bills."

> My students wrote essays for homework this week,
> The usual stuff for grade ten,
> I asked them to write how they'd change the world
> If the changing was left up to them.
>
> His name was Rick Johnson; he was surly and shy,
> A student who's always ignored.
> He'd slouch in his seat with a Malcolm X cap,
> Half-asleep, making sure he looked bored.
>
> His essay was late—just before I went home,
> It was wrinkled and scribbled and thin,
> I thought to reject it . . . (Why do teachers do that?)
> But I thanked him for turning it in.
>
> "You can't cure the world," his essay began,
> "Of the millions of evils and ills,

But to clean up my world so I could survive,
I'd cut Band-Aids and five-dollar bills.

"Now Band-Aids are beige—says right on the box
'Skin tone' is the color inside.
Whose skin tone? Not mine! Been lookin' for years
For someone with that color hide.

"Cause Band-Aids show up, looking pasty and pale,
It's hard to pretend they're not there,
When the old man has beat me and I gotta get
stitches,
Them Band-Aids don't cover or care.

"And now, you may ask, why would anyone want
To get rid of five-dollar bills?
Cause for just that much cash, a dude's mama can buy
A crack rock, or whiskey, or pills.

"She smokes it or drinks it, and screams at her kids,
Then passes out cold on the floor,
By morn she remembers no pain, just the void,
And her kids wish the world had a door.

"So my magical dream is not out of reach,
Like curing cancer, or AIDS, or huge ills,
All I ask from my life is a little respect,
And no Band-aids or five-dollar bills."

Rick and Keisha and Q. and all of the other young people
who sit in our classrooms are all stars—all of them are candles in the darkness, and our job is to show them how to
shine. We must not let their lights flicker or fade. It is our job
to keep their candles bright, intense, and full of hope.

When I was a little girl, my parents saw me as one of
those bright flames of possibility. They nurtured and
shielded me with a protective glass dome so I could burn
brightly without wind or cold to threaten me. My mother
read to me constantly, so that by the time I started school, I

was already an avid reader. Mother would quiz me on spelling tests, and Daddy would check my math facts. My mother tutored me through eighth-grade French without knowing any of it herself. It never even occurred to me not to do well, not to continue to shine. We need more parents who read to their children, parents who will take the time to keep the candle lit.

And we need great leaders—community, business, and educational leaders—who will help us improve our schools, provide us with the wax and the tools to make bright and shining candles that will light the way to our future. One such leader is a man I know who owns a small grocery store—not one of those franchises, just a small, neighborhood grocery. His store is across the street from a school. He offers free bags of groceries to parents who volunteer at the school and he supplies a free turkey dinner to needy families of the children each Thanksgiving. He got involved because a teacher asked him if he'd like to help. We should never be afraid to ask community leaders to become school supporters.

But most important, we need the teachers, the educators—the candle lighters. Teachers are the inspiration and imagination of education. Without them our world would grow dark and cold and the faltering glow from Keisha or Q. or Rick would sputter and expire. Together our lights will be powerful, blinding, and intense.

> This candle is Donna who is hurting and thin.
> This candle is Tina who tries
> but never can figure the factor of ten.
> This candle is Lisa who lies.
>
> This candle is Robert who lives on a farm
> and Leon who lives all alone.
> It's Mona and Alex and Buddy and Kim
> whose gang friends have turned them to stone.

This candle is Aswad and Chengli and Raul
And Kelly and Kathy and Jean
who share the same classroom and same childhood fears
of monsters or hunger or dreams.

This candle is teachers who stay late at night
grading papers or coaching a game,
who never get glory or thank-yous or chalk
but always live up to their name.

If the glow from one candle can brighten a room
the glow from three million can blind!
But when one student smiles and says, "Hey, now I get it!"
That candle makes all of us shine!

So light your candles. And let them shine!

Involvement with Students

Romeo and Juliet

I always try to challenge teachers who are new to the profession to become involved in student activities. It helps you become a necessary thread in the fabric of the society of the school. Cheerleader or track coach, student newspaper advisor, Student Congress director—anything that allows the unique interaction that emerges when students and teachers work together for a common goal in activities that are outside of the classroom.

Several years ago the drama department at school decided to perform a production of Shakespeare's *Romeo and Juliet*. It's probably one of my favorite plays to teach, so I was anxious to see the performance with my classes. I rearranged my teaching schedule so that our reading of the play would coincide with the production, and all of us were excited about it. Several of my students even decided to try out for parts.

When the director announced the date of tryouts, he had a surprise for the whole school. The parts of Romeo and Juliet would be played by students, but the parts of many of the adults in the play would be played by teachers! Tryouts would be open to faculty and students alike. This had never been done before in the history of the school. Several of my students challenged me to try.

"I just like to teach it," I told them honestly. "I don't know if I could perform it."

"You perform it when you're teaching us," they countered. "You're always telling us to reach for the limits and try new things. You chicken?"

They were enjoying this role reversal, and I couldn't find any reason why I couldn't or shouldn't try, so I showed up in the auditorium on the designated day. They cheered when I walked in. Several other teachers decided to take the challenge as well.

The director had us read the parts out loud, with drama and flair, and although I was nervous, I did my best. I left there feeling like a teenager, nervous and unsure of my capabilities. Three days later the list of performers was posted. Two of my favorite students had received the roles of Romeo and Juliet, a physics and chemistry teacher got the part of Friar Lawrence, an art teacher was to play the role of Lord Montague, Romeo's father, and I got the part of Lady Capulet, Juliet's mother! I wasn't sure if I was glad or disappointed. That meant rehearsals every day after school, and lots of time dedicated to study and preparation, time I didn't have enough of BEFORE this started. But I told them I would do it. I savored the taste of the challenge.

We started rehearsals, and the students at first weren't sure how to deal with teachers in their midst. How casual should they be? How respectful? It was a little awkward for all of us initially. But we persevered, and like any cast, we became close. We bonded and formed a unique family as we practiced, rehearsed, goofed up, forgot lines, and gave the words of Shakespeare a spirit and a life on the stage. I was particularly bad at remembering my lines, but the students were so helpful and supportive. I learned things about them that I never would have known without that personal interaction, and they learned things about me as well.

We were fitted for costumes, and I truly felt like a Renaissance queen as I waltzed around backstage in my gown. There was one large changing room for the cast—faculty got no special privileges. Seeing each other in various stages of undress was truly a leveling factor. The kids barely bothered to glance in our direction. We did unity and bonding exercises before the show, and I have never felt so close to any people in my life. We were a cast, a family, a troupe of performers with one common goal.

The show opened with the traditional sword fights (the kids *really* enjoyed that part!), and finally Lady Capulet, the Nurse, and Juliet have their first scene together.

LADY CAPULET: Marry, that 'marry' is the very theme
I came to talk of. Tell me, daughter Juliet,
How stands your disposition to be married?
JULIET: It is an honor that I dream not of. . . .
LADY CAPULET: Well, think of marriage now; younger
   than you,
Here in Verona, ladies of esteem,
Are made already mothers. . . .
LADY CAPULET: Speak briefly, can you like of Paris' love?
JULIET: I'll look to like, if looking liking move:
But no more deep will I endart mine eye
Than your consent gives strength to make it fly.
(Act I, Sc. 3)

Romeo and Juliet is a tale of headstrong teenagers who are trying to thwart parental control of their lives. It's a tale of love and passion and anguish and death, which is why it is so popular with all audiences, but with teenagers especially.

To perform it on stage with young people who are just as headstrong, opinionated, and passionate as the young lovers of Shakespeare's play was truly a delight. We giggled during Juliet's death scene but made it look like heart-wrenching tears, and we rose to heights of drama, heights I never knew I could reach.

LADY CAPULET: He is a kinsman to the Montague;
Affection makes him false; he speaks not true:
Some twenty of them fought in this black strife,
And all those twenty could but kill one life.
I beg for justice, which thou, prince, must give;
Romeo slew Tybalt, Romeo must not live.
(Act III, Sc. 1)

For a few brief moments, I really *was* Lady Capulet, angrily and passionately calling for the death of the young man who had just killed my nephew. It could have just as easily been a headline in a newspaper today—the outrage caused by a senseless death in the streets of the city.

And the arguments between parents and child? So very contemporary. Parents who love their only daughter, feeling that they, as adults, are the only ones capable of making sound decisions about her life, and the teenaged daughter, causing extreme consternation to her parents, rebelling and refusing to obey their wishes. So much of what we teach from long ago relates to the lives of our students today.

LADY CAPULET: Marry, my child, early next Thursday morn,
The gallant, young and noble gentleman,
The County Paris, at Saint Peter's Church,
Shall happily make thee there a joyful bride.
JULIET: Now, by Saint Peter's Church and Peter too,
He shall not make me there a joyful bride. . . .

CAPULET: Doth she not count her blest,
Unworthy as she is, that we have wrought
So worthy a gentleman to be her bride? . . .
Thank me no thankings, nor proud me no prouds,
But fettle your fine joints 'gainst Thursday next,
To go with Paris to Saint Peter's Church,
Or I will drag thee on a hurdle thither. . . .

JULIET: Good father, I beseech you on my knees,
Hear me with patience but to speak a word.

CAPULET: Hang thee, young baggage! disobedient wretch!
I tell thee what: get thee to church o' Thursday,
Or never after look me in the face. . .

LADY CAPULET: Talk not to me, for I'll not speak a word:
Do as thou wilt, for I have done with thee.

JULIET: O sweet my mother, cast me not away!
(Act III, Sc. 5)

The students felt the power and the passion of those words. As teachers and parents of teenagers, we could understand as well. At the end of the performance, the audience gave us all a standing ovation. My world expanded that year, and I learned about myself as a teacher of young people, as a teacher of Shakespeare, and as a teacher of life. Those students involved were changed and expanded as well. The interaction we had with the students in that production will be remembered long after essays or lectures in class are forgotten. That is the essence of education.

There's No Such Thing as "Just a Teacher!"

Pride in Our Profession

I'm a teacher. That is what I AM. That is what I do. I'm good at it, I'm proud to be what I am, and I'm proud of what I do. I'm very proud to be a teacher. Pride in our profession is essential—and that message must be shared through all levels of our field.

I was asked to speak at a university recently to a group of preservice teachers. They were eager with anticipation, hopeful, and terrified. When I asked for questions, one young lady raised her hand and voiced what many of the others were afraid to say out loud. "What do I tell my friends," she began, "when they ask me why I want to waste my time in college learning to be just a teacher when I could do so much better pursuing another career?"

I smiled and told her, "There's no such thing as 'just a teacher!' Don't EVER think of yourself as JUST a teacher! There is no such animal. You are so much more than that. Look at your hands—those are the hands that will determine the fate of the twenty-first century! That is not exaggeration or rhetoric—that's the truth." I told them then to think back to the teacher or teachers who made a difference in their lives, and I watched their faces as they smiled with the memories those teachers evoked.

Then I told them, "Next time you're at a party and you are feeling intimidated by the 'professionals' who give you their business cards, whip out your card, on which you have inserted 'Mary Jones—EDUCATOR,' and remind them that none of them would be the professional success they are without real good teachers in their past."

On another occasion, I asked a group of business professionals about the teachers in their past, and the difference those teachers made in making their lives successful. They, too, nodded in assent, except for one rather belligerent gentleman dressed in the obligatory black suit and red tie. "I can't think of one teacher that made a difference in my life," he asserted loudly from the back of the room. "I can't even remember the name of even one of them. My teachers were weak and forgettable—all of them!"

The audience waited for my response. I asked the gentleman quietly, "Can you read, sir?"

"Of course I can read!"

"Then you can thank a teacher!"

When I was honored at the White House in April of 1997 as recognition for being named the 1997 National Teacher of the Year, President Clinton looked up from his prepared script, looked wistfully into the past, and named every single one of his elementary school teachers. He knew them all, and remembered them with pride and pleasure. He reminded us how important the role of a teacher can be in the shaping of young lives.

I met one of those young lives recently in Denver. I was the invited author for their Right to Read Week. I gave my presentation, read glibly and cheerfully from my books, and spoke to those children as if they were my own students. Dozens of children surrounded me afterwards, giving me hugs and asking for autographs on little scraps of paper. In the midst of the confusion, I felt a tug on my jacket and heard a little voice say, "Miss Book Teacher! Miss Book Teacher! I can't REACH you! I can't REACH you!"

I turned around, and there stood a tiny little five-year-old determined to capture my notice. I gave him a hug and the attention he demanded. But I thought about what he said.

- If we can't REACH the five-year-olds in this country, we can't teach them.
- If we can't REACH the adolescents in our middle schools, we can't teach them.
- If we can't REACH the potential gang members, or teen mothers, or drug abusers in our schools, we can't teach them, and we can't make a difference in their lives.
- If we can't REACH the legislators of educational policy and reform in this country, we can't teach them—and yes, they need to listen to the teachers—so that we can make a difference in the lives of the students.
- If we can't REACH the parents and business professionals in the community, we can't teach them, and we can't show them how they can make a difference in the lives of the children.
- If we can't REACH the teachers, to tell them of professional development, and certification, and forums, and technological connections through the Internet, we can't teach them, and they can't reach the students they have been given.

It's all about reaching and teaching. When I first started teaching, an elderly black woman who had retired after thirty-five years of teaching took me aside. Her name was Mrs. Brady. She said, "Honey, you're going to be a great teacher. But you've got to reach 'em if you're going to teach 'em. If you remember these things, you'll be just fine:

- Don't just teach these children—love them as if they were your own, and they will love you back.
- Remember that their world is bigger than yours because they live in it every day. You are an interruption to their lives. Find your place in it.
- Teachers teach not just subject matter; they also teach life. Let your students see the rainbows of life through you.
- The golden rule seems to be fading these days, but it's not yet made of clay. Treat your students with dignity and respect and they will treat you the same.
- Success always works better than failure. Children who feel successful will try again tomorrow. Children who feel like failures will give up, and tomorrow they will be discipline problems.
- Don't expect miracles. A miracle might take a lifetime, and you only have until the end of the bell.
- And wear comfortable shoes! This is no time to be cute!"

Several years ago a diminutive but antagonistic seventh grader got into a fight almost every day. He was bright but so very angry. Any word or comment would set him off. He seemed to almost enjoy fighting—he would start a fight by his words, or incite a fight by his actions. No one ever got the last word on Monty. But his constant suspensions and punishments were affecting his school work, and Monty was doomed to fail at seventh grade and at the rest of his life if nothing changed. We couldn't REACH him.

The principal and I called his parents on numerous occasions. His mother didn't live with him, but his father, a brusque and forceful-sounding man, always seemed very angry that Monty had once again been disciplined for fighting. Finally, we told the father that Monty could not return to school until they came in together for a conference. We almost dreaded the day when we would finally meet Monty's father.

He arrived exactly at 3:30 and demanded loudly of the secretary, "Where's the principal and that teacher?" She pointed toward the principal's office and excused herself to get a cup of coffee. She didn't want to be near the fireworks.

Monty Senior stood well over six feet tall. He was unshaven, had heavy work boots, and wore a thick brown leather bomber jacket. Monty Junior, a scant four feet tall, for once was quiet and obedient as he huddled silently next to his father. The principal ushered them into the office and the four of us sat down. Eyes glaring, Monty Senior listened to the infractions and problems of his son. Monty Junior squirmed uncomfortably in his seat.

I ended with a demand that sounded more like a plea. "Monty has got to stop fighting, sir."

"Why?" Monty Senior replied curtly.

"Because that's not appropriate behavior, sir," I replied.

"I don't see it that way," he replied. "I told him to fight. Told him that I would beat him up if he didn't fight. That's the only way he's gonna learn to be a man, the only way he's gonna live in this world!"

The principal and I were silenced for a moment. She got up then, went to her desk drawer, and took out a tape measure. She walked slowly and deliberately to Monty Junior and silently began to measure him. Vertically. Horizontally. Silently. He looked at her as if she were crazy, and so did his father.

Finally the father spoke. "What you doing?"

"Measuring your son, sir."

"For what?"

"For his casket, sir. You see, if he doesn't stop fighting, one day soon someone will decide fists are not enough and they will decide to shoot him. So I just want to be prepared, so we'll know what size casket to order for him." She sat down. This time it was Monty and his father who were shocked into silence.

Finally Monty Senior spoke. His voice had lost some of its gruffness. "I don't want him to die. I love my boy. I just want him to be a man."

The principal spoke softly. "Your son will be a fine man, sir. He's intelligent, he's handsome, and he has so much potential. He looks to you, sir, for guidance. Help him to live to be the man you want him to be."

Monty Senior looked at his son. "You cut that fighting out, boy, you hear me!"

Monty Junior, relieved to be removed from the center of a crisis, mumbled, "Yes, sir."

From that moment, Monty's behavior made a noticeable, if not drastic, improvement. His father occasionally showed up unannounced at school, "just to check" on his son. Monty's grades and outlook on seventh grade improved. By reaching both Monty and his father, we were able to teach both. Two lives were saved that day by reaching out and reaching beyond.

No, there's no such thing as "just a teacher." Teachers save lives on so many different levels. But we can't teach them unless we reach them.

One Class

Thirty Reasons Why You Teach

1. Sophie Robertson has a cold. She has sneezed all day and you know you're going to get sick. She's pale and always ill. She has ten brothers and sisters. Her coat is thin and her shoes well worn. She rarely smiles, so you give her a hug in spite of her cold. She looks up at you with bleary eyes and smiles brightly. She sneezes again.

2. Lisa Martin brought you an apple. You hate apples and this one was bruised and slightly mushy, but this was the first time in all your years of teaching that a student brought you an apple. You cherish it, but you don't eat it.

3. Benjy Zimmerman fell during recess and scraped his knee. Benjy has had seven injuries at school this year. He's a little clumsy, but he likes the attention that bandages bring him. You have forms to complete in triplicate.

4. Vicky Zimmerman, Benjy's twin, fell during gym and scraped both knees. She always has to do whatever

Benjy does, then beat him by one point, even on spelling tests. More forms to fill out in triplicate, again.

5. Anissa Logan needs to wear her glasses. You have to call her mother again before you go home. You suspect that she has been hiding her glasses because she thinks the boys won't like her if she wears them. Anissa has been complaining about headaches and she squints all day.

6. Keith Holbrook has read seventy-two books this semester. You worry about challenging him and giving him activities to keep him stimulated and excited about learning. He's read all the Tolkien books, every single Stephen King book, and he's asking you for more. He'll be eleven next week.

7. Sara Thompson is addicted to jelly beans, as well as anything else that is made mostly of sugar. Her teeth and her weight both show it. The other kids tease her, which makes her eat more. You've tried talking to her, even called her parents for a conference, but they are not concerned. Sara is very unhappy and you worry about her. She brought you a bag of caramels last week.

8. Chris Gardner sells candy to everyone before and after school. He brings a book bag full of candy that he buys at a discount store. Then he sells it to his friends for a higher price. He has lately expanded to notebook paper and pencils. He always has cash on hand and is generous with money to students who need lunch money. He tells you he could sell drugs just as easily, but candy won't send you to jail. Chris will be rich and successful, probably before he leaves high school.

9. Michelle Morris told you proudly yesterday that she won the Miss Junior Model contest and will be absent

for two weeks to go to Texas for the finals. She is often absent for modeling assignments and beauty pageants. Her clothes are more expensive than yours.

10. Stella Smith has a learning disability. You've been trying for three months to get testing services to return your calls. She reads words, and even sentences, in inverted order. Her comprehension skills are excellent when the material is read to her, but she wants to be, and needs to be, independent. She's often frustrated and cries easily. You remind yourself to call testing services one more time.

11. Kevin Thornton just transferred in last week. His family moved from California. He's good-looking, friendly, and carries an air of self-confidence. The girls are attracted to him because he's new, which is why the boys dislike him. You like him because he loves math.

12. Sam Lee is so shy and withdrawn he's invisible. He never plays with the other children or joins in class discussions. He keeps his head down whenever possible. His handwriting is so small it is hardly readable. Your efforts to draw him out have failed. He whispers when he talks.

13. Jerome Jones told you last week that he wants to be a teacher. He said his father told him to think about being a doctor, but he said, "Blood turns me off." He told you he wanted to teach because his teachers had always "been cool with him," so he figured he could do that too.

14. Curtis Simpson has cystic fibrosis and is absent more days than he is present.

15. Mike Boswell has sickle-cell anemia and is absent more days than he is present. Mike and Curtis, who

have bonded because of shared illnesses, share a home tutor and computer games. They once did a report together and told the class about hospitals, doctors, tests, diagnoses, and their diseases. The class shows both boys lots of respect and consideration, and helps them with missed assignments when they return from an extended absence.

16. Carla Cosgrove is probably sexually active at age eleven. You've seen the older boys hanging much too close to her after school. You can see her future, and you don't know how to save her. Carla's mother is twenty-three.

17. Dora White loves to argue. She's the class champion of unfair situations. If a student is unhappy because a seat was changed, Dora will plead the case. When students think they deserved a higher grade, they get Dora to help argue their cause. Dora knows she wants to be a lawyer. She carries a briefcase.

18. Precious Truelove is not much like her name. She disagrees with everyone and picks fights just to have a reason to fight. She was suspended twice in the first month of school. The counselor told you yesterday that her father is suspected of abusing her. Her mother is in jail for prostitution.

19. Lillian Ling recites a poem every day just before the dismissal bell rings. She has three fat notebooks of stories and poems that she has written, and she's never afraid to share them. Her parents come to every school event, even though they speak no English.

20. Rufus Wilson knows the statistics of every basketball player in the NBA, but he's failing math and reading. He tells you he won't need that stuff because he's go-

ing to be in the NBA. He's tall, strong, and dreams only of basketball.

21. Ray Byles tells you that the principal plans to implement block scheduling—next week. Ray's mother works in the main office. You don't fight it; you adapt—just as you do to the fire drills in the middle of tests and standardized tests in the middle of a project on Egypt. You learn another lesson about flexibility.

22. Kelsey O'Doul's mother stops by your room after school just to say thanks. Kelsey finally understands math, and even likes it! She tells you that you have made a difference in her daughter's life. You are amazed, and humbled.

23. Jackie Thompson is a social butterfly, tending to everyone's needs but her own. She collects friends like other children collect stickers. Much of Jackie's world is invented. She tells stories of wild parties and adventures in New York. She lives with her grandmother, who is very strict. She has never been to a party. She has never been to New York.

24. Monica Murphy was abused as an infant and lives with foster parents, whom you suspect abuse her as well. She sits in the back of the room and refuses to remove her coat, even in warm weather. You have tried to talk to her, but she refuses to open up to you. She bites her fingernails until her fingers bleed.

25. Daryl Dothan knows more about computers than you do. He learned to surf the Net before he learned to swim. He fixes the classroom computer whenever it has problems; he even increased its memory. He promised to fix the error in your hard drive next week. He's ten.

26. Report cards are due in two days and you have misplaced the bubble sheet to record the grades for the school computer. Before you find it you get a memo saying the school computer is down and grades will not be due for another week. You decide not to tell them about Daryl Dothan's computer skills.

27. The new blackboard you ordered for your classroom five years ago arrived today. They tell you the board will be installed during class time because after school would be overtime for the installers. You've never been paid overtime, but you're thankful for the shiny new blackboard. Christine Ellerby, who plans to work construction with her dad, watches with fascination as the board is installed.

28. The physical education teacher stops by to tell you that Veronica Kennedy, the fastest runner in the school, has just been diagnosed with bone cancer. She may never run again. She may lose a leg. You wonder why.

29. Justin Washington, who has never received any public praise or recognition, blushes with pride as you give him an extra copy of yesterday's newspaper. He was featured as "Student of the Week" as a result of your nomination.

30. Your students gave you a surprise birthday party last week. They gave you handmade cards and a bottle of the cheapest perfume you've ever smelled. Several cards said how much they liked you. Three children said they loved you. And one card said, "You're really OK for an old person."

These, and hundreds of reasons just like these, are why we teach. We make a difference, one child at a time.

Power

The Power to Dream

A reporter once asked me, "If you could eliminate anything in American schools today, what would it be?" I ask you the same question. What would you get rid of? Overcrowded classrooms? Bureaucracy? Lunchroom duty? That kid in the third row?

You know what I told him? I told him I'd get rid of failure. No child would ever fail. Nobody would ever be labeled with an F (like the woman in *The Scarlet Letter*) and branded as inadequate or lacking. Every child would know the power and joy of success.

I remember such a child—one who had rarely received any better than a D on any report card. He was tall, gawky, and never smiled. He was decidedly not good-looking. His clothes were old, worn, and sometimes dirty. He felt like a failure—and many of the teachers, I'm sorry to say, treated him like one.

One day at lunch I asked a veteran teacher, a woman whose bronzed hair never moved and whose outfits always matched, "How is Tom Turner doing in your class?"

"That dirty little Tom Turner is a pain," she replied. "I hate having to even look at him."

"I'm sure he feels the same about you," I commented dryly as I ate my tuna sandwich.

If no child ever failed, then no schools would fail. If no schools ever failed, then our society will feel that same power and joy of success. We would have finally created an alternative to failure—one that allows only successful learning experiences, one that allows the children to dream. And how can we accomplish this impossible task? Through teachers. We have the power. That teacher had forgotten her power, her ability to change things and to make a difference.

We have the power to create quality schools in which failure can be eliminated and dreamers can be nurtured. We have the power to develop well-trained, professional teachers who know how to make a difference in the life of a child. We have the power to encourage the best and brightest of our students to enter the field of education. We have the power to become mentors, leaders, and keepers of the dream. We DO have the power!

Do you believe it? Do you feel it? It's hard to feel the power when your classroom is overcrowded and underlighted, when your supplies run out long before Christmas vacation and your requests for assistance go unheard. But the power exists. Hidden under the minimal paycheck for your maximum effort lies the power that gets you up each morning and keeps you coming back. That power lies in the faces of the children. The children who need success to succeed. The children who need teachers to reach that success. Yes, we have the power to work with "other people's children"—the power to make magic, make miracles, make dreams come true.

Most teachers can probably remember the one teacher who had the power and who used it with skill, the teacher who most greatly influenced them to become a teacher.

The teacher who showed me the power of teachers was my fifth-grade teacher, Mrs. Kathadaza Mann, a strong black woman who taught us to be proud of our heritage as well as our capabilities. She was undoubtedly an early influence on my love of learning and teaching. Mrs. Mann was truly powerful—boldly speaking for those of us who did not yet know how to speak for ourselves. She taught black history long before it was politically correct or socially acceptable, and loved all of her students, both black and white. From her we learned so much more than math and spelling. She challenged the accepted standards to prove to us we were wonderful, and we believed her. And she read literature to us—Shakespeare, Thoreau, and Dunbar—and we loved it and learned it because no one ever told us we couldn't. She gave us the power to dream. I wrote this for her on the day we met again, thirty-five years later.

Teacher

I was ten and full of wonder
Anxious then for school to start
With red plaid dress and brand new crayons
Fifth grade dawned to grab my heart.

Our teacher met us at the door
How low and silky hummed her voice
A mystery of books and chalk dust
She offered challenge, change, and choice.

She wore pearls and silky dresses
Laughed and cheered each sweet success
Marched with us to higher visions
Never stooped or stopped for less.

Cloakroom hooks and home for lunch time
Days of hot and cold extremes
Games for math and bees for spelling
Fifth-grade memories, magic, dreams.

With a smile she taught us patience
Whispered secrets breathed us strong

Words and rhymes and tales of beauty
Filled our minds with joy and song.

Through her wisdom we dreamed visions
Of fruits of pride and hope's moist vine
Because of her life, I am a teacher
Touching lives as she touched mine.

In high school I had other powerful teachers who taught me to love poetry, music, and art, and those who taught me to read analytically, to think critically, and to speak fearlessly. It was those teachers who encouraged me, by their example and by their power, to try to make a difference in the world.

But much has changed since I was a student in school. Finding the power and wielding it effectively is often close to impossible. Today, capturing the attention as well as the spirit of the contemporary student is a difficult task. Children of the nineties have grown up with momentary video images with much sound and very little substance. They are frenetic, energetic, and restless; channel surfers in all aspects of their lives—busy and constantly bombarded with stimuli from radio, television, and computers. Adolescents rarely take the time, or even have the patience, to sit quietly and read even a newspaper, let alone a book. To share the power with them, we must first get their attention.

One young man who needed attention, direction, and power stands out vividly in my memory. His name was Leon. He was almost fifteen, a unique young man who was intense and nervous and excited about learning. And he had SO much to learn! He really tried to please. He had transferred from a school in Canada, where he was encouraged to be expansive and creative, but never focused or analytical. Also, he was never corrected for grammar or punctuation—he said his papers were only graded for "originality of thought." Because part of the stated purpose of this class was to prepare students for the writing skills necessary for college, sometimes the really creative students felt stifled. Leon's writing style was as large as his handwriting, and he and I had trouble agreeing on how to focus on analyzing literature, but he was always willing to try to adapt himself to what I asked of him.

Early in the school year I asked him to write a literary analysis of irony in Steinbeck's *The Pearl*. He didn't like the book at all. He said it was "interesting, original, and a bit stupid," and stated that it had a "sappy ending." Speaking of sappy endings, he ended his paper with, "I would recommend this book to a person who was completely bored out of their gored." He usually wrote the first words that popped into his head, whether rational or not. But in spite of the really rough structure of the paper, it showed possibilities of power, if only that power could be captured. For example, he said, speaking of the pearl, "Instead it brought him anguish, death to loved ones, damage to the one valuable possession that he has, and his home burnt to ash." He followed that beautiful statement with, "But this book was stupid because of the dialogue."

In conferences with Leon, I started slowly. I pointed out to him that good writers don't usually analyze literature by calling the work "stupid." In another composition, he discussed the symbolism of *A Separate Peace*. Although the paper was a little convoluted, he showed hidden depths of analytic ability. He said, "The tree reflects on the war because the tree was youth and when they jump from it they leap into manhood which war would change you to." The idea that the "tree is youth" and the "leap into manhood" are wonderful examples of creative expression that needed direction and focus. I continued to conference with him. He even asked for extra time after school, where he really tried to understand what all this "analysis stuff" was all about. He finally wrote in another paper, "This story used powerful

irony, in many cases some of which are very hard to find."
But at least he had found a glimpse of the power. Leon will
be a success story one day. That's all one teacher can hope
to do. Pass on the power. Feed the success rather than the
failure. It seems so insignificant, but that is truly a miracle.
We must ensure that such miracles continue—one child at a
time. We have the power.

Butterflies and Possibilities

The Story of Tony

One July afternoon a group of three hundred teachers stood outside on a hot sunny day in Alabama. Classes for the year had been over long enough to have begun to fade into memory and classes for the new school year were in the future, a vision not yet formed. We had come together to speak of possibilities, of what we could accomplish as educators as a whole. In our hands we each held gently a small paper pouch. Fluttering delicately inside each small paper prison, a butterfly hovered, waiting for release.

We looked to the sky and saw the glory of the day, felt the warmth of the sun, and dreamed the hope of the next generation. Each of the butterflies represented one child, or ten children, or ten thousand children to come—not as they are, but as the possibilities they can become if given the freedom and boost they need.

At the given signal, we opened the packages and raised our arms to the sky. The butterflies, instead of emerging neatly and orderly like released helium balloons at a carnival, were hesitant and confused at first. After the darkness of their confinement, many refused to leave their pouches. They huddled in a corner and had to be coaxed with gentle words and gentle puffs of breath on their wings. Others crawled slowly to our hands and fluttered there, gathering strength and purpose, enjoying the warmth of the day and the safety of the moment. Only a few flew confidently and strongly toward the call of the sky at the moment of their release.

The children in our classrooms are much the same. Some are prepared and ready to go to the next level with very little help from us. We call those our success stories, but actually those students would have been successful without us. The true successes are the students who need to be prodded from their shelters of ignorance and apathy, encouraged and gently nudged toward their destination, until finally, after much difficulty, we watch them fly away successfully.

I remember one such butterfly. His name was Tony. He walked into my classroom on the first day of school with a frown and an attitude. He was sullen, withdrawn, and negative. He never joined in class discussions, rarely did his homework, and always did poorly on tests and other class assignments. He made it very clear that he hated school, hated English class, and hated me, but not necessarily in that order.

I tried everything. I encouraged him with smiles. I challenged him, dared him, teased him, cajoled him—nothing worked. I called his mother many times, so much that we got to know each other fairly well.

"I'm having a problem with Tony in class."

"I know, but don't give up on him. He's got so much potential!"

"Yes, but his 'potential' is getting to be a problem."

"I'm going to keep working with him at home. You keep trying at school."

"Yes, but when does Tony begin to try to make it?"

"He's gonna make it. You'll see."

The year continued with very little improvement. His attitude and approach toward class affected the whole atmosphere of the class. The usual relaxed, cheerful feeling that I liked to maintain in my classes had been replaced by tension and dissention. The conflict finally reached the breaking point.

I was walking around the room, collecting homework, chatting with each student for a moment or two as I picked up the papers. I approached Tony's desk. His defiant eyes dared me to speak to him. I took the dare.

"Where's your homework, Tony?"

Instead of the usual "I ain't got it," he spewed a filthy stream of curse words at me, indicating his disgust with homework, with school, and with life in general. The class got deathly quiet.

Now I was a fairly young teacher, and I'd never encountered such a situation. I was overwhelmed at the idea that a young person could contain so much venom. I really had never heard such an intricate string of expletives. So I made a fatal mistake. I said with disbelief to Tony, "What did you say?"

So he repeated himself. Louder this time.

I rarely have to remove students from class, but I had no choice but to ask Tony to leave. He viciously grabbed his books, slammed the door, and stomped down the hall. The rest of the class finally exhaled and we continued the lesson, but not very effectively.

Tony was suspended from school for what the kids called "cussing out the teacher." When his suspension was over in a week or so, Tony chose not to return to school. In December of his senior year of high school, Tony quit school. I felt like such a failure. Whatever potential he might have had was forever lost. But school continued, his class managed to graduate quite well without him, and the next school year, as well as the next, rolled along its never-changing cyclic path. But I never forgot Tony. Some students live with you forever.

Two years after that explosive afternoon, I got a phone call.

"Hey, Ms. Draper, remember me? This is Tony!"

"Of course I remember you, Tony. How could I forget? How have you been?"

"Oh, I'm working, getting myself together. I think I'm ready for college now!"

"That's good to hear, Tony. I always knew you had potential."

"Uh, that's why I called. Could you write me a college recommendation?"

I was silent for a moment. "Sure, Tony, but I'll have to tell the truth!"

"Oh, they've seen my record. I'm gonna have to prove myself. I just want you to tell them about my potential."

I wrote the best recommendation letter I have ever composed. I concentrated on his potential rather than his past, and he was admitted. He never wrote me or called me from college, but I heard from his friends that he had moved to several different colleges, and that he had gone to the army. The years rolled along. Fresh fall days, winter storms, spring mud, summer vacation, and back to school again. Tests, attendance, papers, successes, and failures. Never the same, always the same. Ten years had passed from the time that Tony cursed me out in sixth bell.

It was February and I was teaching *Macbeth*. Almost

on cue with the knocking at the door of Macbeth's castle, I heard a knock at my classroom door. Mildly annoyed because of the interruption, I opened the door, preparing to get rid of whatever student envoy was selling balloon-a-grams or raffle tickets. Instead I faced a familiar stranger—a tall, handsome soldier in his dress uniform. Perfectly groomed with shoes shined and creases precise, he carried in his gloved hands a single red rose. It was Tony.

"This is for you," he said simply, as he handed me the rose.

I took the rose, tears burning my eyes in spite of myself. "Where have you been, Tony?" I asked finally.

"I just got back from Desert Storm," he said. "I've seen war, and it's awful."

"What did you do there?"

"My job was to count and photograph the Iraqi dead. Then I had to put them into body bags."

I gasped.

"I grew up while I was there," continued Tony. "I thought I was grown long ago, but I was wrong. So I just wanted to see you now that I'm home, and I wanted to thank you for what you tried to do for me, and I want to tell you that I'm sorry."

I let the tears fall this time. I gave Tony a hug, introduced him to my class, who could not possibly understand what was going on, and then he left. I have not seen him since.

I still have that rose, however. It is dry and distorted between the pages of an encyclopedia, but it is one that I will treasure forever. Sometimes it takes years to make the connection between student and teacher, years for the butterflies to find the strength and courage to fly in the summer sun. Rarely does one of them come back to thank you.

I ran into Tony's mother at the grocery store not long

ago. We exchanged greetings, chatted for a moment, and I asked, "Now how is our Tony?"

"Oh, Tony's fine. Married. Working. Living in California. Got a son named Tony Junior."

"I am so proud of him," I told her with genuine admiration. "What kind of job does he have?"

"I thought you knew," she replied slowly. "Tony is a teacher. He's teaching high school English!"

Another butterfly had finally flown into the sunlight.

The Needs of Children

"A Wide Sea and a Small Boat"

> "Dear Lord, Be good to me.
> The sea is so wide and
> my boat is so small."

This statement, used by the Children's Defense Fund, reminds us how fragile and dependent our students are. Whether we teach toddlers or high school seniors, they are pawns in a world they did not make, partners in a game they had no choice but to play. We must remember that children are just that—children. They're not small adults or incomplete pieces of protoplasm. They're kids. They need to laugh and giggle and make mistakes. They need to pretend. They need to dream.

Whether the children are underprivileged and have never seen the inside of a shopping mall, or overprivileged and are given so much they have very little left to desire, they all have dreams. They need love. They need to be touched. They need to know that someone cares. Sometimes the only someone to show that care, the only one with whom a child dares to share a dream, is the teacher.

How does one create a dreamer? Through creativity and imagination. By allowing a child permission to "color outside the lines." By encouraging questions and fostering thought. By creating an atmosphere where dreams can grow and blossom.

What about the children who have failed, not just in school, but in life, the children whose dreams have been destroyed in the dirt? Perhaps these are the children that illustrate the failure of society. I once visited a school that wasn't really a school—it was a jail. These children, ages ten to fifteen, had committed crimes—crimes so heinous that they could not be returned to their families, but had been placed by a judge in this facility for criminal children.

To enter the building, I had to pass through two sets of security checks. Then I was ushered into the bright, colorful reception area. Student-made posters adorned the walls, as in any school. But I saw no students. I was told they were in their cells. "Cells?" I asked. "Yes, cells," I was told.

I was taken on a tour of the facility by a large and cheerful guard. The library. The cafeteria. The gym. It looked like any other school. But it wasn't a school—it was a residential correctional facility. There were guards here, and locked doors, and no access to the outside.

They showed me the rooms where the children slept. Small, bare, almost antiseptically clean. A small bunk with a single mattress, a sink, a toilet, a shelf. And a door with no doorknob that locked from the outside. It was a jail cell.

The children were to meet with me in the area that was used for cafeteria and assemblies. Three rows of folding chairs sat empty, waiting for the children to be brought in. The guards attempted to prepare me before the children arrived.

"They don't get many chances to hear outside speakers."

"Well, I'm glad I'm able to be here for them."

"When they do get a speaker, they usually last about fifteen minutes, and we have to take them back."

"Oh, I thought I had an hour to speak to them."

"You won't last that long. These are really rough

characters. But don't worry, we've put on extra guards. You'll be safe."

The "rough characters" were marched in then. Single file. Heads down. Hands clasped behind their backs. A guard in the front. A guard in the back. Totally silent. They sat down quickly in what seemed to be preassigned seats with none of the shoving or the usual jostling that accompanies children when they come into an assembly that is exciting simply because it breaks the normal routine. They were being taught correct behavior and had learned not to deviate from it. They did not smile. They wore white T-shirts, dark sweat pants, and slip-on sandals. No shoes with strings.

Guards flanked them on either side of each row. Several more stood at the rear of the rows. They hovered closely, checking for even minor infractions of the rules. They gave me the sign that I could begin.

I looked at the rows of silent faces in front of me. One little boy had freckles and bright red hair. I smiled at him and he smiled back shyly, but not before quickly darting his eyes to the guard standing near. Another boy, with a head full of curly black hair, looked at me like any seventh grader looks at a new teacher—a mixture of doubt and anticipation. Every single one of them looked like kids in any middle school in the United States—kids with adolescent pimples, kids with braces, kids who leave their book bags on the bus. Not criminals.

The first thing I did was to make the guards move back. I wanted to talk to these young people, and I felt no threat from them. I did not know what crimes they had committed. I didn't want to know. All I knew was that they were kids and they were hungry—hungry for praise and a little positive reinforcement.

I started out by telling them stories—stories about some of the people I had met and some of the humorous events during my travels. The stories made them laugh, or reflect, and removed them from their own lives. They didn't have to think about themselves for a few minutes, and both laughter and tears are wonderful relaxers.

One story was about a young man I met at an airport. He carried a map of the airport, an old duffel bag, and one long-stemmed red rose. He asked several people questions, and looked nervous and anticipatory. I watched him for a moment. Then, when he boarded the shuttle train to head to the baggage claim area, I spoke.

"Got a special girl waiting?"

"Yes, ma'am. Is this the train to get a cab? I'm in a hurry."

"Yes, this shuttle will take you to that gate. I'll show you when we get off."

"Thank you, ma'am." He glanced at the rose again, smoothed the wrinkled paper around it, and checked his watch once more.

I couldn't help myself. The boy was about the age of my son. "She must be a very special young lady," I ventured.

The young man smiled then. "Oh no, ma'am. This rose isn't for a girl. It's for my grandma. I ain't seen her in three years."

"Is she sick?" I asked.

"No, ma'am. She's just fine, but I just can't wait to see her. It's been so long."

"Have you been away at college?"

"No, ma'am. I've been in jail."

He was such a fresh-faced kid, so young, so innocent-looking. He could easily have been in my class last year. "Are you glad to be home?"

"Oh, yes, ma'am! I ain't never going back there no more. My grandma raised me, and she tried to tell me stuff about going to school and staying out of trouble, but I wouldn't listen. So I just want to go see her and thank her and tell her I love her. She's all I got in the world."

The shuttle stopped then, and he bounded off to head for a taxi. "Give your grandma a hug for me!" I called to him. He turned, grinned, and promised he would.

Many of the children I was speaking to on that day had been raised by grandparents. I could see the look of fond recollections on their faces. Then I told them about Zak.

I was tired and frustrated. I had spent several hours in the Charlotte airport because of a cancelled flight. When the plane was finally ready to board, I asked if I could get my seat changed from an aisle to a window. All I wanted was a quiet spot. I dragged myself on the plane, hoping, in spite of the screaming babies all around, that I could just lean my head against the window and sleep for a few minutes.

When I got to 12A, a little boy was sitting there, next to his grandmother. His arms and legs, obviously badly burned, showed many scars of multiple grafts and layers of mottled skin.

"Hi, I'm Zak."

"Hi, Zak," I replied gently.

"Is this your seat, ma'am? Zak wanted to ask if he could have the seat by the window," his grandmother said to me.

"Sure, Zak, take the window. I love sitting in the middle seat."

"I'm five years old today! You know, I was four yesterday, and today I'm five! I don't see how that happened! I was four for such a long time. I was getting tired of being four, and now I'm five. It's about time!"

"Well, Happy Birthday, Zak. Enjoy sitting by the window. Where are you from?"

"I'm from Conway, South Carolina, and I just got back from Cincinnati."

"Cincinnati?" I asked the grandmother.

"He goes to the Shriner's Hospital there. That's where he gets the treatments for his burns. He got burned when he was eight months old—grabbed a cord of an electric frying pan and pulled hot grease all over him. Sixty-eight percent of his body was burned. Praise the Lord his face got spared, and his groin area—(them Pampers don't burn!), but the rest of his little body was almost destroyed."

She told me about the private jet that the Shriners sent to pick Zak up when he was burned, how he was burned at 8:00 P.M. and by 1:00 A.M. he was in Cincinnati in treatment. She told me how he was not expected to live, but they tried some new treatments and he rallied. They fly back and forth from South Carolina to Cincinnati on a regular basis for his grafts and treatments, and all of it is paid for by the Shriners Hospital. I have lived in Cincinnati all my life, and never knew what a wonderful job they do with kids like Zak, who was charming, energetic, and learning to fight unbelievable obstacles in his young life.

I forgot how tired I was, and was ashamed of myself for complaining about such mundane inconveniences as a late plane flight. I told Zak I was a teacher, and he was fascinated because he was going to start school in the fall. We talked about school for a bit, and I told him what he could look forward to, like reading, and making friends. He was quiet for a moment, and then he said to me, "You get to talk to a lot of kids in your job?"

"Yes, I get to talk to young people all over the United States—even South Carolina."

"Well, when you get a chance, would you tell them something for me?"

"Sure, Zak. What would you like for me to say?"

"Tell them to be really careful around fire."

"I will, Zak. I promise."

They understood about kids with problems. They understood about obstacles. They sat rapt and fascinated, while I told tales and gave them subtle encouragement. Forty-five minutes had passed. The guards made no move to end the session. Finally, I asked the young people for questions.

They wanted to know about my school, my students, my children at home, my age. (Kids always ask that one.) Then finally, the red-haired, freckle-faced boy in the front row raised his hand. He asked me the hardest question I have ever been asked, even by the best Washington and New York reporters.

"If you could give some advice to us in here," he began, "what would you tell us?"

The room was silent. Never had I faced such a difficult question. I thought for a minute, then took a deep breath.

"Tell them to stay in school," I heard a voice whisper behind me. It was the director of the facility. The kids heard it, and I saw their shoulders visibly slump.

"I'm not going to tell you what your director wants me to say," I said slowly, ignoring the director's snort of disapproval behind me. The kids sat up straighter, listening. "I'm going to tell you something that will last a little longer." Even the guards were rapt with attention.

"You cannot change your past. What has happened to you, and what you have done can never be changed. It is the past and it is gone." They were with me, their faces reflecting their thoughts.

"Your present is not very pleasant, but it is a place where change can take place. It is a place where decisions can be made and wounds can be healed. It is a place of transition." They were starting to move uncomfortably in their chairs.

"Your future is a glorious rainbow if you want it to be. You have the power to make your future anything you want it to be. You have the strength within yourselves to create your future. Never let anyone or anything remove that from you. You have the power to fly!"

I could tell by the looks on their faces that they believed me. Many of them had tears in their eyes. Most of them shook my hand when it was over. Some gave me hugs. They needed the warmth of another human being. The guards marched them back out to their cells then, again single file, hands behind their backs. But as they left, they held their heads up high, and they smiled at me as they marched out of the door.

The Gift of Time

Of Heroes and Hopes

If I could give teachers everywhere one gift, it would be more time. There's never enough time. Not enough time to grade the papers and fill out the forms in triplicate and prepare lessons and go to meetings. Not enough time to stop by the cleaners and the grocery store and the post office before it's time to pick the kids up from the bus stop. Not enough time to teach vowels or long division or honesty or fair play when that child that touched your heart moved away just as you were making the connection. Not enough time to please the principal and the parents and your spouse and your children. Just not enough time.

What time does the bell ring? Do I have time to stop by the gas station, the ATM machine, the coffee shop—before school? Do I have time to call each parent of my one hundred and fifty students between the time school ends and the faculty meeting begins? Do I have time to fill out the report cards this weekend? Do I have time to fill out the detention forms? Eat lunch? Go to the bathroom?

Where did the time go? Just moments ago, you were

starting out as a student for the first time in kindergarten, wide-eyed with wonder, some of you tearful, some confident, but excited at the possibility of new horizons. Your teacher spoke gospel and time was your servant then. Days stretched for endless hours of play and imagination. Time was punctuated only by meals or naps or new adventures. School was fun—and easy! You never even thought about your teacher and how he or she managed to have such colorful and topical bulletin boards, or new songs for you to sing, or new materials for you to discover. It never occurred to you the amount of time your teacher spent in preparation for your edification and inspiration.

Somehow you woke up just a few days later and you were in seventh grade, awkward, gawky, faking confidence, clinging to time, refusing to let go of those times of childhood, hesitant to challenge the treacherous times of puberty and maturity. Your teachers had become plural and their world existed on a plane far removed from the private world of self-absorption reserved for adolescents. The extra time your teachers took to coach the baseball team or tutor you in math was swallowed without thanks.

In high school you were still the master of time. You were learning the difficulties of managing a life, but the horizon was far distant and the possibilities were limitless. The freshman says, "I've got plenty of time." The sophomore responds sardonically, "Who cares about time?" The junior is starting to feel the pressure, but avoids it by saying, "I still have time to get it done, to get it right, to get it together." The senior starts to panic, realizing, "I'm running out of time." All of a sudden the teacher, and the teacher's time, are valued a bit more, and many wishes and pleas are made about chances to be given more time.

Suddenly you find that time has transported you to today. Now you ARE the teacher, and somehow the places have been reversed. Time has propelled you from that first day in kindergarten to today, and the innocence of childhood has been replaced by the taskmaster of adulthood, a ticking clock.

Each phase of life is a learning experience for the next phase, which moves us on to the next. You no longer belong in kindergarten or seventh grade. You belong to the world now—to the cycle of growth and development and change. And you have a responsibility as well—to make a difference in at least one life: to be a hero to someone who needs you.

Do you remember the story of Beowulf? Beowulf was the ultimate hero. He was a hero supreme—courageous and powerful and handsome, sung of in tales and legends in his own lifetime as being "the bravest and strongest man of anyone, anywhere on earth." He had the strength of fifty men, fought sea monsters and dragons. He was invincible.

He had the strength of thirty men, and boasted about it. Nobody on earth could beat him, and he knew it and so did everybody else. He came in to Hrothgar's land, killed the monster and swaggered away, the young, victorious hero—champion of all. He ruled his own kingdom for fifty years then, noble and wise and loved by his people. But when the dragon attacked his land, he needed a young hero to help him, because the cycle of time had slowly turned and Beowulf, the ultimate hero, could no longer defeat monsters alone. But in his lifetime, in his moment of shining glory, he made a difference in the lives of others. He took the time.

And to give the women equal historical opportunities, let me remind you about Boudicca, the fifth-century Celtic princess who gathered an army of Celts and defeated the more powerful Roman army. Boudica was a hero, a powerful maker of the destiny of her people. But soon she also was replaced by the next generation of warriors and leaders. But she made a difference, oh what a difference that red-haired princess made in the lives of her people. She, too, took the time.

Each season brought new challenges, new adventures, and new obstacles to overcome for Beowulf and Boudicca. Each season brought new monsters and new maidens. So it is with teachers. Each of us is a hero, fighting ignorance and apathy, bureaucracy and despair. And every season we are given a new group of challenges, with different faces but similar problems. We take them by the hand, lead them around the path of the cycle, and take them to their next destination.

Beowulf was indisputably powerful, but teachers are not usually thought of as powerful people. We are taken for granted by society, just as we tend to take ourselves for granted. We say to others, with a sigh of resignation, "I'm just a teacher." Would Beowulf have called himself "just a hero"? Would Boudicca? Beowulf dared anyone NOT to call him a hero. We must do the same. For the cycle is ever-moving, and the next semester of challenges will be here all too soon.

You, the teachers today, are the heroes, the Beowulfs and Boudiccas of our generation. You are the champions, the dragon-slayers, the men and women who are the makers of the destiny of all of us here today. What will you do to effect a positive change in the lives of the children you teach? What will you do with the time you have been given as a gift? Will you be a hero?

Suppose I gave you $86,400 as a gift? What would you do with all that money? Now suppose I added a condition to my gift—that you must spend all of the money tomorrow. All of it. Could you do it? There's more. On Tuesday I shall give you another $86,400, with the only condition being that you must spend it all on Tuesday. If you do, I will give you another $86,400 on Wednesday, with the same condition, and again on Thursday, and Friday, and Saturday, and so on. After a while, you'd beg me to stop, because you just could not spend all that money.

Guess what? Each day of your life is made up of 86,400 seconds. And every day you are given that gift new and unspent. Each day you have the opportunity to spend that gift of time. And you can buy anything you want with it. What will you buy?

We take time for granted. We are given 86,400 seconds in each day, 31,536,000 seconds in a year. Do we comprehend the value of time?

I had a student several years ago who found out that she had cancer. She bravely went through treatments, hair loss, and pain. But she never lost her joy in life, her interest in books, her love of poetry. I asked her once how she did it.

"I plan to use every single second that I have here," she told me. "I don't have time to waste. There is so much I want to know and so little time to learn it all."

Lisa ran out of time, and she died at age fifteen, full of knowledge and ready to discover the vast mysteries of the world beyond. She was my hero.

I wrote this poem for another child I know, a young woman with severe disabilities. She could not write it herself, but she understood its essence. Time for her is not a gift but a prison. Her name is Wendy, and she is truly a hero.

> I am Wendy.
>
> I'm a rainbow.
> I am color and light and possibility
> I am hope
> I am lost dreams
>
> I am ageless.
> I am twelve or thirty or sixty—
> Nobody really cares how old you are

when you can't walk
can't talk
can't dance

Sometimes I get tired of can't
Actually, the only thing I *can* do real good
is can't

I want to dance—

I hear the music
I dream the movement
but only in the darkness
of my dreams

I'm a rainbow
Rainbows dance in sunlight
They never sit by a window
and watch time
dance by the door

nobody talks about time here
yesterday is today is tomorrow

Don't feel sorry for me though
don't weep
don't laugh
and don't dream

I dream enough for all of us

last week I saw a rainbow
nobody stopped to notice it
nobody stopped to smile
but I did
I had the time

I'd like to touch a rainbow some day
In a rainbow I could dance.

Time is eternal, but fleeting. It must be spent wisely, carefully, and thoughtfully. For once it is gone it can never be retrieved. What have you done with the hours, the moments, the seconds you have been given thus far? And what will you do with those to come? For the gift I offered you is not hypothetical—it's very real. It is as real as the heart that beats within you. My gift to you is time. Use it wisely. Use it well. You are a teacher. You are a hero. You have the time and the gift to make a difference in the world.

Renewal

Not Quite Burned Out, but Crispy Around the Edges

It was the end of sixth bell on a cold and dreary February afternoon. I stood slumped inside my doorway, glanced at my watch, and sighed as I watched another class of eighth graders troop noisily into the classroom. The joy of the December holiday season had long been forgotten, and summer vacation loomed as an unimaginable speck of hope in the distance. I was tired—tired of the repetition, of the monotony, of the routine of teaching. For twelve years I had told the same jokes, taught the same lessons, given the same tests, and made the same complaints to no one in particular. Something was missing. I sighed again.

When I first started teaching I was full of enthusiasm and excitement, ready to conquer all educational ills. But time and adolescents have a way of draining the energy of even the most ardent enthusiasts, and gradually I found myself succumbing to the dull, meaningless repetition of uninspired instruction.

The teacher across the hall, an older woman who had

taught thirty-five years and still bounced with the energy of a beginning teacher, noticed my depression.

"What's wrong?" she asked.

"I don't know what's wrong," I confided to her. "I feel like I'm in an endless time warp. I can't remember yesterday, and I'm not looking forward to tomorrow."

"So do something about it," she said simply.

"What do you mean?" I retorted. "I show up every day, I teach great lessons, and I don't even know why any more. What am I supposed to do?"

"More," she replied cryptically. "You have to do more."

"I don't even have the energy to do what I do now. How can I do more?" I complained. "I'm here early tutoring kids, and I stay late with the cheerleaders. I can't do any more!"

"That's wonderful, and as it should be, but what have you done for yourself lately?" she continued. "What have you done for your own professional development?"

"Huh?" I wasn't even sure what she meant. "I go to faculty meetings," I said weakly.

"Have you taken an education class lately?"

"You mean on purpose?" I almost laughed.

"Have you ever been to a teacher's conference in another city?"

"Why would I want to go to another city to be with a bunch of teachers? That sounds boring."

She ignored me and repeated her question. "Have you ever been? How do you know?"

"No," I admitted. "I get those notices of conferences, but I throw them away."

She marched back to her room and returned with a colorful flyer. "Fill it out. Send it in. Then go. When you get there go to as many sessions as you can, listen to the keynote speakers, talk to the other teachers there, and take an extra bag with you for all the free stuff you'll receive at the exhibitors' area."

"Free stuff?" I said as the bell rang.

"Bring me a poster." She smiled as she closed her door.

I read the flyer carefully and with great interest. I found there would be sessions taught by other teachers from all over the country. There would be opportunities for great edification, plus some time in the evening for socialization. I decided to go.

I left with great trepidation because I had never been away from my family overnight, but I returned with great celebration. It turned out to be a wonderful experience. I learned wonderful new ways of approaching old material. I learned how to look at problems and accomplishments with different eyes. And I learned that my family could do just fine without me for a weekend. That conference changed my life. I came back with new ideas, new attitudes, and a suitcase full of freebies!

Now, whenever I get the chance, I challenge beginning teachers to join their professional organizations right away and to become actively involved in the activities it offers. By helping yourself grow professionally, you will find that the life of your classroom as well as your personal life will be enhanced. And to those teachers who feel a bit "crispy" and need to be revitalized, active involvement in professional development activities can add the needed spice to a bland routine.

I spoke to a group of teachers in a small Midwestern town who were so discouraged that they were all in danger of severe burnout. This was the first time I had ever encountered a whole faculty that was greatly in need of renewal. A whole audience of crispy, burned-out teachers. A thick fog covered the town as I drove to the school that morning from the dingiest hotel on the face of the earth.

The halls of the hotel were dimly lit, the rooms were worse, and the towels were a dank, dingy gray. It sat right next to the Rocking Rodeo Bar and Lounge, which was right next to the school.

The teachers trooped in, looking haggard and worn, and it was the first day of the school year. I saw no joy, no excitement, no anticipation. Except for two young teachers sitting in the back. I focused on them. I tried stories and jokes and tearjerkers, and most of the faculty sat there, impassive throughout. But the two teachers in the back sat rapt and attentive, grasping my every word. The other teachers sighed with resignation and checked their watches, hoping I would finish soon. But I was determined to reach them. What could have caused such overwhelming collective destruction of their souls?

I asked them finally, "How many of you have been teaching more than ten years?" Most of them raised their hands. "More than fifteen?" The hands stayed raised. "More than twenty?" With the exception of the two teachers in the back, all of them had been there for twenty years or more. They had seen layoffs and cutbacks and shortages. They had dealt with failure and apathy. Except for the two young teachers.

Finally I asked, "Is there anyone here who is teaching for the very first time?"

Shyly they both raised their hands. I was exultant.

"Stand up!" I told them proudly. "I want everyone in the audience to give these two young teachers a round of applause! And I want you to buy them lunch!" The new teachers giggled with embarrassment and pride as they stood to the applause of the others.

I reminded the other teachers, "Take care of these young ones, for they will bring the spark back to you. They are the future of education. If we get more like them, we can all retire!" Finally, I got smiles, even cheers, from the audience! "Let me tell you a story," I told them.

Once upon a time in a town just like your town, but not very much like any town you know, children went to school with joy and pleasure. Their teachers were happy and smiling and the schools bustled with knowledge and adventure. The night before the first day of school each year, children could barely sleep, so great was their anticipation. For on the very first day of kindergarten, each child received a gift—a solid gold coin. It was wrapped in silver cloth and presented to the children with great ceremony. Every child in every grade was given a gold coin on the first day of school. Children took their coins home to their parents that afternoon and celebrated the joy of education. No one asked where the coins came from.

The children had several options as to what to do with their coins. When they graduated from high school, they could choose one of the following:

- Give their collection of coins to their favorite teacher to thank them.
- Give their collection of coins to a first-year teacher to help them get started.
- Keep the coins collected and use them to go to college to become a teacher.
- Take the collection of coins and invest them in the stock market.

Of course, most of the children chose to invest their coins, so the town became not only the happiest town in the world, but also the most wealthy. That generation of children grew to adulthood, married, and the second generation of children soon were ready to begin their adventures in education.

In one household, which was very much like all the others, Misty Morgan tossed restlessly with anticipation the night before her first day of kindergarten. Her parents had told her of the wonderful gift she would receive on the first day of school, and every first day after that. She dreamed of becoming rich like her parents and the parents of all her friends. She also wanted to learn to read. Misty was up before dawn and dressed before breakfast. She wanted to be waiting at the door of the school with her friends before the first bell rang. Her mother kissed her good-bye and gave her a small gold box in which to place her coin. Misty felt as if she would burst with pride and pleasure.

When school was over, Misty walked home slowly, head down, feet kicking the few leaves that had fallen. She walked into her house and went straight to her room. Her mother, who had cookies baking in the kitchen as a celebration, called to her. "Misty! Come downstairs. Tell me about your day. And let me see your coin!"

Misty walked slowly down the steps. "I didn't get a gold coin, Mom," she said sadly.

"What do you mean? The gold coins are always given on the first day!" her mother exclaimed.

"We didn't get coins today," Misty repeated. She dropped the special gold box to the floor. It was empty.

Misty's mother hugged her daughter. "What did your teacher say at the coin ceremony?"

"We didn't have a coin ceremony."

"No ceremony!" her mother replied with shock and dismay. "So did your teacher tell you why?"

"We didn't have a teacher," Misty explained.

"No teacher? Was she sick?" Misty's mother was concerned and confused.

"Nobody had a teacher today, Mom. We watched cartoons in the auditorium all day."

"I don't understand," wept her mother. "What went wrong?"

Misty sighed. "There's no more teachers, Mom. Nobody gave their coins to their favorite teachers. So they all retired. Nobody gave their coins to a beginning teacher. So they all quit. Nobody used their coins to become a teacher. So we don't have any teachers."

The teachers were silent, attentive, intrigued. All of them—not just the young ones in the back.

I continued, "Once upon a time is usually used for fairy tales, but this story could come true. If we don't nurture the teachers we have now and encourage the new teachers who are stepping into place, we won't have enough teachers for the twenty-first century. Take care of these young ones, and don't ever forget the reason why you teach. We teach for the children. These young teachers have not had a chance to forget. Let them help you to remember."

I ended with one last story:

On the outskirts of the same town in which Misty lived, an old man, the oldest man in the town, labored alone near a large chasm. His back was bent with age, and his movements were slow and sometimes painful. But every day he could be seen, cane in one hand, hammer or saw in the other, trudging slowly to the spot near the wide valley. He cleared bushes, moved boulders, chopped trees, and sawed them into planks. Every day he worked silently in the hot sun or the cold rain, oblivious of travelers or distracters. Gradually it became clear what he was doing. He was building a bridge across the chasm.

Misty rode her bicycle to that place one day. She watched the old man work, then asked him, "What are you doing, sir?"

The old man stopped his hammering, looked up at her,

and smiled. "You are the first one to ask me what I'm do ing," he declared.

"So tell me," Misty repeated, "what are you building?"

"I'm building a bridge," the old man said proudly.

"Why?" Misty asked bluntly.

"To build a path to the other side," the old man replied with just as much bluntness.

"But you're old," Misty continued with the honesty of a child. "You won't have much chance to go to the forest on the other side of the valley."

"You're right," the old man agreed with her. He was still smiling. "I'll have very little need and very little reason to ever go across this bridge."

"So why are you building it?" Misty asked. "Isn't that a waste of time?"

"No, my child," the old man replied gently. "I'm build-ing this bridge for you."

The light, as well as tears, had returned to their eyes, and they stood and applauded. They had remembered. And so had I.

Technology

"I Touch the Future; I Teach."

Gigabytes and cyberspace. Internet and CD-ROMs. Hard drives. Software. These are words that my teachers never knew. The world of technology has exploded so fast in the past few years that state-of-the-art equipment that was purchased just a few years ago is now obsolete. Remember reel-to-reel tape recorders? Transistor radios? Manual typewriters? The technology classes I took in college, which were called audio-visual classes then, taught me how to load an eight-millimeter film projector, how to use an opaque projector, and how to splice an audio reel. Only the government had computers, and they were huge, mysterious contraptions that took up entire rooms and completed complicated calculations shrouded in mystery.

Today teachers and their students have access to personal computers—laptops and hand-held—that can compute in seconds the same information that took hours for those bulky boxes to process. We have available in our classrooms telephone systems; sometimes (if we're fortunate) we have Internet connections, video cameras and recorders, televisions, slide projectors, and overhead projectors—and every day more sophisticated devices are being created and made available for our use.

It is sometimes difficult to comprehend the wealth of materials and to know what to do with all of it. Some teachers with computers use them only as fancy typewriters, ignoring the vast possibilities that even one computer in a classroom can offer. Others refuse to touch any piece of equipment that is more modern than a radio, refusing to take the classes that are offered to learn how to implement the new devices in class. Most, however, have embraced the new technology with avid enthusiasm. They write grants for funding of equipment when the school cannot afford it, they share with their students the opportunities for learning that exist, and, if they are wise, they learn from their students the latest techniques, for many of those students come to us knowing more about technology than we ever will know.

Our students today grew up with blow-dryers and microwaves, remote controls and call waiting, and they don't even know what a vinyl record looks like. They have cellular phones and pagers, voice mail and web pages. Fax machines, space shuttle launches, and color copiers are as ordinary to them as applesauce. They live in a world of instant gratification where their needs are immediately fulfilled—money machines on every corner, drive-through food and services, one-hour photographs, and one-minute meals. They expect their world to be technologically secure, and they have grown lax with the luxury that technology affords them.

When my son was about six, we went on a family camping trip. The plan was to return to the beauty of nature by truly roughing it. We were to sleep in tents and sing songs by the campfire as we roasted our fresh-caught fish. Nature can be really rough, however, and we couldn't get the fire started. The wood was wet, the matches were damp, and our spirits were sodden as the constant rain. After dozens of fruitless tries to start the fire, my son turned to his dad in frustration and exclaimed, "Daddy, why don't you just plug it in?" His world was made of electric plugs and artificial lights. It would take much more than a weekend in the woods to unplug him from the items he took for granted and considered to be necessities.

Another time I was teaching in my classroom on a dark and rainy day. Thunder roared and lightning flashed. Students, even seniors in high school, don't like thunderstorms, so they were huddled and quiet, nervously paying less attention to me than to the storm. Suddenly a huge explosion of thunder followed an intense flash of lightning and all the lights went out. Boom! The whole school was dark. All the electricity, all the lights, all the computers, even the phones were off. There was nothing that could be plugged in.

We sat stunned and silent for a few minutes. Then one of the largest, strongest boys whispered from the back of the room, "So what do we do now?"

The class was nervous and upset. I calmed them quietly and said, "Let's do what people used to do before we had all these modern appliances. Let's sit down and talk together." We pushed the desks aside, sat on the floor, huddling closely for human reassurance, and we told stories, we sang songs, we talked and laughed. By the time the lights came back on, we had changed somehow. We had learned that human communication is the most powerful tool.

Americans are spoiled (and I admit I am the most spoiled of all!) and take for granted all the plentiful goods and services we have available. If we have a headache, we can go to any drugstore, convenient store, even gas station ministore, in any city or town in this country, and choose from ten different kinds of headache medicine, with or without aspirin, with or without a buffered coating, in gelcaps or tablet form, from several different chemical formulas, in small, medium, large, or wallet size, and it goes on and on. If we want to record a memory, we have the choice of audio or video, digital or disc, CD or tape, battery-powered or electric, etc. That is repeated for every consumer good and service we desire. And the choices available for technological goods and services are exploding exponentially. This is the world we have created for our children. We must teach them to live in it successfully, yet still remind them of the necessity of living together as human beings without computer connections.

I once visited a class of third graders who were proudly showing me their computer skills. The teacher had them actively engaged with a delightful program, and she scurried around the room, making sure no one had technical glitches. The computer program they were working on gave them bells and blinks and flashing screens when they answered a math problem correctly, and a digitized barking dog when they were incorrect. One little girl sat in front of her screen, oblivious to it all. She was crying. No one had noticed.

"What's wrong?" I asked her. "Are you having difficulty with the computer?"

"No," she replied, wiping her tears and sniffing loudly.

"Did you get a problem wrong?" I continued gently.

"No, I got them all right," she replied, staring at the floor. Her tears were dropping on her shoes.

"Can you tell me what's bothering you?" I persisted.

She looked at me and said quietly, "My mom had to go to the hospital last night, and I'm scared." I gave her a hug and let her talk a minute or two about her fears. I tried to reassure her and she seemed to feel better. The teacher walked over then, assessed the situation, and also gave her a quick squeeze. The child relaxed and returned to the computer screen. All she needed was someone to talk to, a human being to relate to. Computers don't listen very well, and they can't give hugs to make a child feel better.

When we implement computer technology into our classrooms, we need to remember that it is just that—technology. It is hardware and software and plugs and connections. It can't see the needs of a child. That's why we need teachers. Computers are just expensive toys without teachers to implement their use into instruction. The magic of math, the mysteries of history, and the excitement of science can all be taught with depth and creativity through the use of computer programs and the Internet. Through the intricacies of the web students can find literal as well as figurative paths to new knowledge and information. Classes can contact other classes thousands of miles away, they can access libraries in other countries, or they can talk to dignitaries and thinkers from around the globe. The possibilities are as endless as the intricacies of the web. And teachers must be prepared to take their children along those paths and learn together. Those who look behind and see only the past—and those who never change and see only the present—will be those whose eyes are closed and are certain to miss the future.

But let's not forget our humanity as we forge into the technological intricacies of the twenty-first century. We teach because of the importance and necessity of human communication. I met a young woman recently who had just been named her state's Teacher of the Year. She was a teacher who used technology extensively in her classroom. At her recognition ceremony, after thanking all of her friends and relatives, she brought her students up on stage. With tears in her eyes she said to the audience, "And finally, I want to thank these wonderful young people. Because these are the people who call me TEACHER!"

Remember the words of Christa McAuliffe, whose life and death exemplifies our connection to technology, our connection to our students, and our reach into the future.

"I touch the future," she said. "I teach."

The Table in the Teachers' Lounge

A Monument to All of Us

It's the same in all schools—represented by the table that is long and wooden, scratched with pencil marks and coffee stains—dominating the dynamics of the teachers who stop for conversation, or respite, or renewal. It is strong, powerful, and supportive, difficult to move, hard to destroy. It silently listens to the hope and enthusiasm of the newest members of the staff with the same understanding that it gives to those who have graded papers on its slightly lumpy surface for many years.

The older tables have cigarette stains and match burns, and smell faintly of old wax and spilled ditto fluid. Modern teachers' lounges are smoke-free and ditto-free as well, with a neat electronic copier sitting in the corner where the ditto master kings and queens once ruled. A soda or juice machine, perhaps a microwave oven, and several phones are now standard equipment. And computers have finally replaced the old Olivetti typewriters, which gather dust in the storage closet.

At the far end of the table the new teachers sit. They

talk of being overwhelmed with the magnitude of the work load or classroom management problems, of lesson plans that might work. They make marriage plans, worry about babysitters and childcare, and try to balance new families with new jobs. They make mistakes and laugh as they learn. They discover it is not wise to give essay tests for final exams when grades are due in twenty-four hours. They learn not to collect notebooks from all classes at the same time and try to take them home in huge cardboard boxes. They discover that the attention span of a fifth grader is a lot shorter than was explained in the educational psychology textbook. For that matter they discover very quickly that very little from their university texts and theories has direct application to the teaching to which they find themselves assigned. But the talk of the new teachers is full of life and hope and expectation and possibilities. They exult in the process of learning to teach, and the old table smiles.

Sitting together near the middle of the table are the teachers who have been teaching long enough to know the joys, the frustrations, and the shortcuts to success. They know how to turn a volatile situation into laughter, how to make a dull lesson dance with magic, and how to survive the day before Christmas vacation. They have lost the youthful glow of excitement, but it has been replaced with the power of confidence and success. Their conversation is of contract talks and sick leave availability. They balance the lives of their own children at home, who have soccer games and track meets and music rehearsals, with the lives of their students, who have the same. They are sometimes tired, and often beginning to feel frustrated and isolated. They see no chance of advancement or recognition. They can't switch to another job, and retirement is in the distant future. They sigh sometimes as they grade papers to which they know the answers without checking the key. And the old table sighs with them.

At the far end of the table are the teachers who are very close to retirement. Their memories trace at least twenty-five years. They move slower and are rarely stressed or excited about anything new. They've seen it all before—block scheduling, classrooms without walls, educational reform, administrative decisions. They know that they will adapt, adjust, and survive. The best of them teach with authority and power. Former students remember them with fondness and sometimes return for visits—grown up, mature, and often thankful. The worst of them hardly teach at all. They simply show up and wait for their last day. But most of them look back with triumph and satisfaction of a job well done, of children changed, of lives touched. The conversation of the teachers at this end of the table is of retirement plans and disability insurance and the marriages of their children. They are paying college tuitions and give a dollar every week to the teacher who buys lottery tickets for them all. They have moved from the far end of the table, through the middle seats, to the end of the table—where they sit with dignity and pride. And the old table smiles.

The progression around that table has existed for many years, and it will continue long after the youngest and the newest teachers have retired. The table stands as silent witness of the record of the daily fears, joys, and accomplishments of the teachers who sit around it. That table stands as a monument to the dedication of those people who tell the stories of hundreds of students, who have graded thousands of papers, who have rubbed their spirits into the texture of the wood. And because of them, the old table smiles.

Just like everything in life, school activities are a series of repetitions that become meaningful with time, part of a circle that has no beginning and no end. That table represents the well-worn cycle of the life of a school and of a teacher. Let us remember the meaning of the circle that the table represents. Let us exult in its continuity.

Professionalism in Teaching

Formal Notes and Informal Memories on the National Board for Professional Teaching Standards

W hen I first received a letter from an organization called the National Board for Professional Teaching Standards in 1991, I had never heard of it. The letter asked if I would like to participate in a national assessment of the professional development of teachers. I almost threw it away as one of those pseudo-educational advertising gimmicks that sometimes adorn teachers' mailboxes.

But I read on and the content sounded interesting—intriguing—even exciting! Professional assessment? Appreciation of the quality of teaching? Making teaching a profession instead of just a job? This was dealing with issues that I had struggled with for years. I always wanted to have professional respect like doctors or lawyers—but somehow teaching just never quite achieved that level in the mind of the public. Now here was an organization whose purpose seemed to be to do what I had always dreamed of.

After thorough investigation, (my principal told me that I would be in the forefront of the educators of the future), I decided to participate in the process. I had no idea what I was in for. But how hard could it be? I'm the kind of teacher who welcomes visitors or evaluators into my classroom, rather than fears them. I tell them, "Come in, sit down, don't bother us—we're learning in here. You might even learn something yourself." So I thought I was ready to be evaluated.

But no evaluator was to come. I was to evaluate myself. Now this was a novel approach. But I still was thinking, "This will be a snap!" How could I possibly fail if I was doing the evaluations myself?

Then the big box came—and I mean BIG! In it was a large portfolio—with more instructions and details and specific information than I could absorb at one time. I was almost overwhelmed—but the instructions were clear, the goals were understandable, and the overall procedure was conceivably possible to complete successfully. Everything was to be based on a set of standards that had been developed by teachers in my field. Teachers had developed the process and teachers would evaluate my work. I appreciated that concept immensely.

This was to be my assessment instrument for the year. As I began to go through its contents, my initial confidence at the ease of completion began to fade. This looked like it was going to be the most thorough, most in-depth evaluation of my teaching skills that I had ever encountered. I was going to have to videotape my classes several times. I was going to have to keep detailed records of my classroom activities. It would be necessary to write in-depth self-evaluations of my teaching methods and their effectiveness and then write reflections on how I could improve. I was going to have to validate what I taught, how I taught it, how my students learned, if they learned, and if not, then why not. I was going to have to think about what I had been doing almost without thinking for the past twenty years.

It turned out to be probably the most rewarding

experience of my professional life. Not only was there much-needed introspection into my teaching, but I also got to interact with other teachers who were also undergoing this unprecedented process. We shared ideas and methods and tales about former students. We also discussed teaching techniques and curricular issues. It was both stimulating and refreshing to be in a room with not just teachers, but the best teachers in the area. It was noticeable, and it was wonderful.

Working through the components of the portfolio, writing the commentaries as I completed each section, taking the Assessment Center exercises—none of this was the piece of cake that I had envisioned. It was sometimes painful and tedious, but it was also rewarding and exciting. It was a learning experience that benefited all of my teaching that year. I learned more about myself and my strengths and weaknesses as a teacher than I ever have in twenty-plus years of teaching.

Since that time, I became Board Certified with the first group of teachers to be named. I went to the White House, where President Clinton honored us for outstanding accomplishment. I've become a member of the Board of Directors of the National Board. I have traveled across the country, talking to teachers about the National Board for Professional Teaching Standards, encouraging them to participate in this professional and valuable process. But most important, I've learned. I've learned that the best teacher is a learner, and I've learned that teachers are indeed professionals.

The teaching profession can be strengthened and improved by doing just that—treating teachers as professionals. If true professionalism is instituted so that the community, other professionals, and the society in general look to teaching as a respected profession, then the educational process and the accountability of the individuals involved will be greatly improved. And we, as practicing professional educators, must fulfill the expectations of the public by providing quality instruction in an environment that is both supportive and rewarding.

Many restructuring plans have been formulated in the last few years that work to improve standards and quality in all areas of educational development. One such avenue of improvement has been developed by the National Board for Professional Teaching Standards. I have been actively involved with the National Board for the past eight years, and I truly believe that the goals and ideals of that organization are one answer to some of the major concerns of educational reform.

The mission of the National Board for Professional Teaching Standards is to establish high and rigorous standards for what accomplished teachers should know and be able to do, to develop and operate a national voluntary system to assess and certify teachers who meet these standards, and to advance related education reforms for the purpose of improving student learning in American schools. Although the National Board cannot single-handedly transform schools, it can be a significant catalyst for change. It can add a new level to teacher education studies. It can offer new incentives to current teachers, entice new and qualified people into the field, and decrease the loss of quality educators. It can become a pathway to improved student learning. It can also hold promise for a reversal in the long-term trend of declining minority interest in teaching.

A national certification program that reliably identifies teachers who meet high and rigorous standards can elevate the entire system. The absence of a credible and accepted method to recognize outstanding teaching sends a message that good teaching is not valued, and that the profession does not take itself or its responsibilities seriously. Certified teachers will acquire and deserve respect and admiration from colleagues, administrators, and the community as well.

The expertise that teachers bring to the education of America's children depends in part on the nation's expectations for accomplished teaching.

The National Board has set high and rigorous standards and a means to achieve and certify those standards in practice, and it has identified and recognized those teachers who have done so. Many of the other major standards initiatives in education are using the premises and principles of National Board standards, producing even greater levels of teacher accountability and student achievement. All of the new standards plans, regardless of philosophical background, strive for increased student learning, improved teacher preparation and practice, and enhanced accountability among education professionals.

If we wish to produce new quality teachers, we must use only the very best and most qualified master instructors to guide and nurture quality in the next generation of teachers. To achieve this optimum synergy, one suggestion might be to implement the skills and strengths of those teachers who have been certified by the National Board for Professional Teaching Standards. These teachers are skilled, passionate, and committed.

- They know their subject matter and how to teach it.
- They are committed to students and their learning.
- They are capable in managing and monitoring student. learning.
- They think systematically about their practice and learn from experience.
- They are members of learning communities.

Board Certified teachers are given both the responsibility and the opportunity to strengthen and improve the teaching profession. But what happens *after* certification? Newly certified teachers come to me and say, "Wow! I'm

Board Certified! Now what?" I tell them that certification is not an end—it's a beginning, a chance to use the best of their skills in an arena much larger than Classroom 102. This is what I tell them:

You've been congratulated and celebrated by your supervisors, your colleagues, and your school. You might have been mentioned in the local media. Your family and friends are proud of you. Most important, you are proud of yourself because you know you have reached a personal milestone of professional achievement. You attempted the process of Board Certification, struggled through the intricacies of the portfolio, and emerged victorious and personally satisfied for a job well done. But what does Board Certification really mean? What can you DO now that you have been designated as an accomplished professional?

Let's start in the classroom, venture outside our classroom door, move to the realm of the entire school, then boldly go outside of the school into the community, into the political arena, and finally return to our classroom—where we find our greatest strengths and satisfaction.

"Hey Miss Johnson! It's like cool you got that certification thing you was workin' on all last year. See what I'm sayin'? But like, what do you do now? You gonna leave us now that you all that?"

"No, Ricky. I'm not going to leave you. Board Certification is a recognition of good teaching. It is designed to recognize and encourage good teachers to stay where they do their best—right here in the classroom. I'm here for you!"

Your students have been involved with you from the beginning. Share your success with them, explain what it means, allay their fears, and encourage them to talk to you about what certification means to your life and to theirs. They are justly proud and also probably fearful that your success will mean you will move away from them. Talk to them openly and encourage them to share your conversations with their parents. Talk to the parents at open houses and conferences and explain to them so that they too have a clear understanding of what the National Board is, and what it means to your school.

As you move outside your classroom door, talk to your colleagues and tell them about your Board Certification experience. Encourage them to become involved, and then be ready to help them when they frantically call you for help (and they will!).

Other things you can do within your school include speaking to other teachers at a faculty meeting or giving a mini inservice to interested staff members. You can talk to administrators and explain to them the importance of their support as teachers go through this process. Remember that not everyone is at the same level of understanding. Start with where they are, and take them to where they can feel comfortable. (Isn't that what we do with our students?)

As you venture out of the school building to speak to others who are not necessarily educators, start with the parents of your students and let them lead you into the community. A father who works at a bakery or a mother who works at the local grocery store can provide you with a connection to the business community. Local bakeries can provide donuts to your students as well as support for teacher candidates. All you need to do is ask. The worst they can say is no. Most business leaders want to see improvements and reform in our schools, because that will ultimately provide better-prepared employees for them. One group of candidates got a local business to match available funds, and twice as many teachers were able to try for certification.

What about colleges and universities in your area? Do they provide support for candidates? Classes for candidates that offer course credit? If not, why not? Someone has to suggest the idea to the curriculum planners at that organization.

Have you approached your local school board? Have

you ever been to a school board meeting? Have they ever given you any award or recognition? Write them a letter and ask them why not, or ask to speak at the next meeting. School boards want the teachers in their district to be successful. Sometimes we need to remind them of the successes that do exist.

That also includes your state school board. They are more than just a governing body far away in your state capital. They are the people who are working for you, and they are anxious to hear of teachers who have accomplished great tasks. Call them. Make an appointment to address them. They will be pleased, proud, and honored to hear your story.

And make it just that—your story. Tell everyone you speak to what the process of Board Certification is like and why it is important to you and to all teachers as well. Tell them about the importance of education on the local level—in your city, your building, your classroom.

The National Board also has lots of activities for you to become involved in. You may be offered opportunities to work as an assessor, as a trainer, as a leader of a local forum, or as a spokesperson for future candidates. If the opportunity arises, take advantage of it. Each situation will be a learning experience, and the personal and professional growth that you will experience from your participation will be immeasurable.

How many politicians have you spoken to? Your state political representatives—and your national senators and representatives—can be powerful allies for you and for education. They, too, need to reminded of the realities of the classroom teacher. They make decisions about us every day. Let's let them know about the positive experiences that are occurring.

Speaking of positive experiences, the news media is notorious for printing only the negative news about schools and teachers. Let's give them something positive to write about. If you don't call them and tell them your story, how will they know to report it? And don't just send a press release. They get thousands of those a day. Write to the reporter who has a regular column, who does "human interest" stories. You'd be surprised how willing they will be to come and talk to you and your students.

If you are asked to speak to a group of strangers, a group of people who are not intimately familiar with the local schools, and you feel a little bit intimidated or unsure of yourself, try this technique. Think of each of them as a student. The big guy in the back who is looking bored. What would you do if that were Billy in the fourth grade? Would you be afraid to get Billy's attention by drawing him into the classroom activities? Of course not. What if someone asks a question to which you don't know the answer? Doesn't that happen in class? What do you do? You laugh and say let's look it up, or you encourage Molly to go and find the answer herself. If you treat each situation as a "teaching" situation, you can handle anything that arises with no trouble. We are accomplished professionals, right? Use the skills that we use every day. That is our strength.

That's our strength because we are teachers. We love our students, love our subject matter, and are skilled in making knowledge come alive in the minds of young people. From this intense classroom experience, we can expand our world beyond the classroom to influence our community, our state, and our world. But it all comes from and ultimately returns to our classroom. Everything that we do is for the children in our classroom today and for those future students who will follow. Because of you, the beacon of education is burning brighter. Share that light with someone today. You can do it. You're Board Certified!

Now, because of this process and the potential that it holds for the future of teachers and education, when people at a party ask what I do for a living, I don't have to respond that I'm "just a teacher." I'm proud to be a teacher—and I'm proud to be a National Board Certified Teacher. Like the scholar in Chaucer's *Canterbury Tales,* now, more than ever, I can take pride in being a learner as well as a teacher— "And gladly wolde he lerne, and gladly teche." And with apologies to Chaucer, and a bow to feminism—"And gladly would she learn, and gladly teach!"

AUTHOR'S NOTE: For more information on the National Board for Professional Teaching Standards, call 1-800-22-TEACH or locate on the web at *www.nbpts.org.*

Teaching and Writing

The "Draper Paper" and Beyond

I have been a teacher of literature and composition for almost thirty years. I have learned as I taught, for I feel that an active learner is the best teacher. That knowledge is something that my students and I affectionately call "the big picture." I tell them that if they learn nothing else in my class, I want them to understand that a powerful connection exists between historical and cultural events and the literary creations of the time—that the art, music, poetry, and prose of the Renaissance, for example, are directly related to the social, religious, and political events of the time. Or, as another example, that facts the students learn in a history class in third bell are connected to the music they sing in fifth bell, which are all connected to the poetry they read in seventh bell. It's hard for students to get cultural perspective unless someone takes the time to show them the links. Sometimes I can see the little light bulbs over their heads as they blink and grin and say with surprised pleasure, "Oh yeah, now I get it!"

I remember one year my eighth graders did a unit on

mythology. After we finished the traditional Greek and Roman mythology, which is pretty standard in most schools, we decided to investigate mythologies of other cultures. We focused on creation myths and looked into cultures as diverse as Egyptian, Chinese, and Babylonian. We found wonderfully creative stories, outlandish tales, and an amazing similarity in all of them. The students delved into the cultures, finding music and literature and art that had a thread of cultural symmetry through them all. They wrote their own myths, and they talked about current cultural myths that we still hold. (The aliens from Roswell sparked the greatest interest and proved to be the best characters for modern myths!) My students had fun, and they learned so much more than any of us ever thought possible.

I have a relaxed, comfortable teaching style. I like the students and they know it. I demand the best from them, and they expect the best from me. We read literature, discuss ideas from the books as well as from world events, and we write. I tell parents that although I cannot guarantee a Rhodes scholar by the end of the school year, I can guarantee that their children will have improved in their writing skills. I once had a student enter a writing contest, and she showed me a draft of her essay. I looked at her quizzically and asked her why she had done such a poor job on it, because we had done that kind of paper many times in class, and her writing was exceptional. She looked at me with amazement and replied, "Oh, I thought that stuff you taught us was just for English class. I didn't know we had to write like that all the time!" My work continues.

When I started teaching seniors, I worried about how to handle them at the end of the school year. By February, if not sooner, they all had a bad case of "senioritis," so they needed something to motivate them and direct their minds until the very last moment of the very last day of classes. Big order. Seniors want to go to the mall or the park—not the library—on a warm May afternoon. So I figured out a way to send them where they least wanted to be—the library!

Seniors at our school were required to write a research paper, and most teachers did it first or second quarter to get it out of the way. I decided to do the project—a full-length research paper of ten to twelve pages with footnotes, bibliography, and all the accompanying bells and whistles—during the last quarter of the senior year. Not only that, but the paper was to be the ONLY work of that quarter, worth more than one thousand points. (The number of points turned out to be wonderfully impressive and added so much to the mystique of the assignment.)

Students, who complained noisily throughout the whole process, enjoyed moaning about the rigors of "that Draper Paper." Each week a step in the research process was assigned, checked, and completed in class. We spent hours in the school library; we took field trips to the downtown library. We learned about card catalogs and the Reader's Guide to Periodical Literature, which are both now basically obsolete, and about computers and shelves and stacks and sources and citations. Gradually they moved from knowing nothing at all about their chosen subject to becoming experts in one small area of knowledge. They knew the names of the recognized experts in their field, bemoaning repetition in sources and information. "Everybody quotes Nancie Atwell!" complained a student who did her research on middle school education. Three weeks earlier, she had never even heard of Nancie Atwell.

They went to the library on their own on weekends, working for hours diligently digging out details, in spite of the warm weather and temptation to be elsewhere. One Saturday I went down to the library and took little bags of jelly beans to every student I found working. They beamed in surprise and appreciation. I ran out of candy. Of course they all crowded downtown the following week in hopes I would show up with treats again.

They gradually compiled their information and prepared a paper of which they could be proud. They sweated over margins and spacing and computers that ate data or typewriters whose ribbons always failed at midnight. We went over proper form for citations and they labored over every dot and comma, as well they should.

Finally, the paper was due, just before the prom, which was always held on Memorial Day weekend. They could relax at the prom, with the major event of the semester, of the year, of their academic life, in my hands, not theirs. They felt triumphant and victorious, especially when, as they handed in their papers, they received their student-designed T-shirts that proclaimed, "I survived the Draper Paper!" Younger students in the school looked at them with awe and respect. They boasted and flaunted, with legitimate pride, of an awesome academic accomplishment, and made sure the younger students were properly terrified of the prospect of getting Draper as a teacher in the coming years. And so a legend was born.

The paper wasn't difficult but time-consuming; it wasn't impossible but inconvenient for a teenager who would rather play than study. What it became was a rigorous, meaningful study that students at first dreaded but later treasured. Many students have returned over the years to thank me, to tell me how they used the paper in college, how it helped them in later academic studies.

The Draper Paper even made national news. When I went to the White House as National Teacher of the Year, President Clinton mentioned it in his speech about me. He said that he had asked me for a T-shirt but had been refused because he had not actually completed the paper. Headlines the next day said, "Teacher of the Year Refuses to Give President a T-shirt." My mother called me and asked, "How can you refuse such a request, dear?" I had never really said he couldn't have one, and I think he said it jokingly, but nevertheless my class that year had a special T-shirt designed for President Clinton and sent him a letter telling him that we were giving him one because of his dedication to educational improvement in this country.

I've always encouraged my students to write, whether it be stories, or essays, or research papers. Many of them were even published in various student publications. But even though I knew intuitively exactly what to do to make their writing sing, I had never taken seriously any attempt of my own to write. However, one day a student came up to my desk with a grin and a challenge on his face.

"You think you so bad," he began, smiling, "why don't YOU write something!"

"I just might do that," I replied.

"Then do it!" he answered triumphantly. He handed me a crumpled application for a short-story contest.

I glanced at it, took it, and told him, "OK, you're on! I'm going to go home and do this!" He didn't think I would, and I wasn't sure I could, but I was ready to try. I stopped by the grocery store on the way home and in an aisle filled with green beans and applesauce I saw a young mother screaming and cursing at a three-year-old child, who cowered in terror at her words. I said nothing as she left the store, still yelling at the child, who looked at her with love and fear. But I couldn't get that child out of my mind. What kind of life did he have at home? How was he treated in private when he was so abused in public? I grieved for him. Although I hadn't planned to, when I got home that evening, I sat down to write, and two hours later I had a story. I wrote it from my heart.

I called it "One Small Torch" and I sent it in to the contest, with my students' blessings. Two months later I received a phone call from the head of *Ebony Magazine,* telling me that my story had been chosen from several thousand entries, as first-prize winner. I was flabbergasted. I got a check for $5000, my story was published, I got my picture in the local paper, and all of a sudden, I was a writer! Even more amazing was a letter I received from Alex Haley, who wrote me, in his own handwriting, a letter saying how he thought I had great talent as a writer. Now that was awesome! So, my students challenged, what are you going to write next?

Since I've been an English teacher for almost thirty years, I know what kids like, what they will read, and what they won't. Although I have nothing against Charles Dickens, most teenagers would rather gag than read him. Dickens wrote for his contemporaries—young people of a hundred and fifty years ago. That's one of the reasons he was so popular—he wrote for his contemporaries! American kids, of course, need to know about the world of London in the 1860s, but they would much rather read about their own world first. Not only will they read about recognizable experiences with pleasure, but they will also be encouraged to write as well. I started my writing career for those young people.

Tears of a Tiger was written in study hall, on weekends, before and after school, and during summer vacation. It is written for high school students—on their level, in their style, about their world. It's written for all teenagers. The characters are just ordinary kids trying to get through high school. The book does not deal with drugs or gangs or sex. It does, however, deal with parents, girlfriends, and homework. It also discusses the problems of drinking and driving, racism, and teen suicide. I sent it to twenty-five publishing companies and got twenty-four rejection notices. The very last letter was a letter of acceptance from Simon and Schuster. We had a real celebration in school that day!

While I was waiting for that one to finish the publication process—it takes about a year and a half—I wrote another book for younger students. It is called *Ziggy and the Black Dinosaurs,* and is written for boys ages six through twelve. This one was accepted on the very first try. *Ziggy* is a funny mystery that deals with club houses and buried treasure, and it even includes a strong lesson on history that young readers learn without even knowing it. The response was so wonderful that I made it into a series. In the second book, Ziggy and his friends find an old, abandoned tunnel of the Underground Railroad and get lost in it. It's called *Lost in the Tunnel of Time.* The third book in this series is called *Shadows of Caesar's Creek* and deals with the cultural connections of Native Americans, again through humor, excitement, and solid literary development. Kids can read this series and learn as well as enjoy the tale. Teachers can use these to teach.

Although it was not planned that way, both *Tears of a Tiger* and *Ziggy and the Black Dinosaurs* hit the bookstores on the very same day! The response was tremendous and overwhelming. Parents have asked, "Where have you been?" Kids are clamoring for the sequels. Schools are starting to adopt them in their curriculums. I don't think I have ever had a young person read *Tears of a Tiger* who did not like it. Actually, many of the teenagers who read it tell me they have never read a whole book before in their life, but they read that one in one night.

Tears of a Tiger has received wonderful reviews, several national awards, and was awarded the Coretta Scott King Genesis Award, as well as being selected as an ALA Best Books for Young Adults for 1995. Amazing for a first book. Two years later I wrote the sequel, called *Forged by Fire,* which is a powerful piece for young people on child abuse and survival. It won the 1997 Coretta Scott King Award as the best book published that year for young people by an African American author. It also won several other awards, but it is close to my heart because Chapter One of *Forged by Fire* is "One Small Torch," the story that won first prize in that short-story contest! My literary success has truly been a dream come true.

I learned to be a dreamer on my mother's lap. She read to me long before I could walk or talk and continued to do so long after I started school. I became a voracious reader, gobbling up books by the dozens each week at our local library. But by the time I was eleven, I had read just about every single book on the children's side of the library, and was given a special pass to check out adult books. By the time I had finished high school, I had read most of those as well. So of course when I went to college, I majored in language and literature and composition.

At the time, I didn't know that the knowledge and ideas gained from all that reading would become the knowledge base for my writing years later. When I write now, the words gallop from my fingers, sometimes faster than my conscious thoughts, and always faster than my fingers. Writing is thrilling and exhilarating. I'm a poet, a creator, a visionary. I approach the world with the eyes of an artist, the ears of a musician, and the soul of a writer. I see rainbows where others see only rain, and possibilities when others see only problems. I love spring flowers, summer's heat on my body, and the beauty of the dying leaves in the fall. Classical music, art museums, and ballet are sources of inspiration, as well as blues music, dim cafés, and the jitterbug.

I love to write; words flow easily from my fingertips, and my heart beats rapidly with excitement as an idea becomes a reality on the paper in front of me. I use all of these elements to encourage my students as well as myself. I'm a learner and a seeker of knowledge, and I take my students along on my journey. I smile often and laugh easily, and I weep at pain and cruelty. I learned to dream through reading, learned to create dreams through writing, and learned to develop dreamers through teaching. I shall always be a dreamer.

I feel very blessed that I have had so much success in such a short time. It makes me smile. A good teacher smiles while she's teaching. She smiles because she is comfortable not only with her subject matter, but also with her classroom and her students. She smiles because children respond quicker to encouragement rather than disparagement. And she smiles because at the end of a very long day, with papers to grade and forms to fill out and meetings to attend, a child may peek his head in the door and say, "We gonna write poems like that again tomorrow? That was fun!" That is when I smile.

Students ask me now, "So you gonna quit teaching now that you're a hotshot writer?" I tell them with a smile, "Goodness, no! I'm just getting started with you! We've got 'miles to go before we sleep.' You're my inspirations. Let's write something together!" And we do.

National Teacher of the Year

So Proud to Be a Teacher

People often ask, "So how do you get to be the Teacher of the Year anyhow?" A few years ago, I would not have been able to answer that question. I never had any great plans to grow up and be the National Teacher of the Year. I remember once seeing a glimpse of a teacher in the Rose Garden of the White House and wondering vaguely to myself, "How did she get to do that?" I bet I could do that, but I didn't have the foggiest notion how. I remember also reading about a National Teacher of the Year flying in Air Force One with the President. Wow. That's the kind of thing that happens to other people in other states. No one we know ever does wonderful things like that. Until now.

It all started very simply. It was May of 1996. The principal of my school handed me an application, about twenty pages in length, that said on the front cover, "Ohio Teacher of the Year—1997." He said, "Why don't you try this?" I shrugged and said, "OK, why not?" I had no notion of where that short conversation might lead. I had no grand plan. I filled out the application, which was thoughtful, requiring broad thinking and a good writing style.

I have since found out that many states do the application process quite differently. In South Carolina, for example, a local winner is chosen from every single school in every single city. The winner of the City Teacher of the Year is announced at a breakfast and celebrated at a formal dinner with gowns and tuxedos. Then that teacher's application goes to the county level, where the process is repeated, and then finally to the state level. All this is a wonderful idea and should be emulated. It gives a glorious opportunity for dozens of teachers to be recognized, celebrated, praised, and lauded as they should be. They are given plaques, or certificates, or golden apples, and they go back to their classrooms refreshed, renewed, and rededicated.

But in Cincinnati we simply fill out the application, and someone in the central office picks a candidate to go to the state competition. In '96, they picked me. I think there were about six candidates. I got a phone call in June, telling me my application would be sent to the state. I was pleased, but I still had no sense of destiny. Shortly after school started in September, I got another phone call. I had been selected as one of the four finalists for Ohio Teacher of the Year!

On October 24, I was in the middle of sixth bell, teaching Chaucer to my seniors. The door to my classroom opened. In walked the principal; the assistant principal; several secretaries; the hall monitors; every teacher with a free bell; the superintendent of Cincinnati schools; the head of the school board; John Goff, who was the State Superintendent of Education; half a dozen reporters snapping photos; other reporters with bright lights and video cameras, and my husband, Larry, with six of his students! Needless to say I was at a loss for words. John Goff said, "Let me be the first to congratulate you as the 1997 Ohio Teacher of the Year!" My class went wild. The kids cheered. I grabbed my face in a gesture of surprise, and lifted my arms as if to say, "Wow!" That picture, in full color, appeared on the front page of the *Cincinnati Enquirer* the next day, covering almost the whole top half of the front page. I drove down the street, just marveling at my picture in those little newspaper stands, over and over and over!

Everyone was so supportive and so genuinely glad for me. The lady at the cleaners, the man at the drugstore, and the tellers at my local bank all stopped what they were doing when I walked in the door to clap and cheer. Everyone felt proud to share my success. I was a part of the community, and I had made them all stand tall with pride. I was overwhelmed and humbled.

Being named Ohio Teacher of the Year was plenty for me. I still had no great dreams of heading for the national competition. The Ohio Teacher of the Year is a position of great responsibility, as are each of the State Teacher positions. I would travel all over the state of Ohio, speaking to teachers and educational organizations, but would still continue teaching. It promised to be an exciting year. But the application of each State Teacher of the Year is passed on to the national office, for consideration to be National Teacher of the Year.

I was certainly no greater than any of those fine teachers, any one of whom could have been chosen. One evening in January the phone rang. It was Jon Quam, the director of the National Teacher of the Year program. He said, "I'm calling to tell you that you have been selected as one of four finalists for the 1997 National Teacher of the Year, and to ask you if you would like to accept this opportunity." Now this was the first moment where I started to get giddy, to look to the future, to imagine the possibilities. I grinned at the phone, told him "Yes, of course, I'd be honored" and other sorts of correct phrases, and hung the phone up and screamed with delight.

From that time until March, when the four finalists would meet the National Teacher of the Year committee, I studied; read *Education Week*; met with people in the educational field here in town whom I respected and admired, such as our Superintendent of Education, Mike Brandt; and read as much as I could about all aspects of education. For now I was not only seeking to speak for the teachers in Ohio, but for all of the three million teachers in this country. I needed to be familiar with all aspects of the educational spectrum. I wanted to be knowledgeable, secure, confident. I had to prepare a ten-minute presentation for the committee, which is made up of fourteen members of the educational community representing the major educational organizations such as the AFT, the NEA, the National School Boards Association, and so forth.

I flew to Washington, D.C., the first week of March. For three days the four of us who were finalists were put through the pace—interviews, press conferences, dinners, videotaping, a presentation, questions about education. It was thrilling, stimulating, exhausting, and probably the best educational process I had ever experienced. They sent us home then with a promise to call us in a week or so. I came home feeling confident, but not overly so. There is just no telling how committees make decisions behind closed doors.

We had been told that if we were NOT selected as the National Teacher of the Year, we would receive a phone call from Jon Quam, the director of the program. If we WERE selected, we would receive a call from our State Superintendent of Education. In Ohio, that was John Goff. Either way, I would get a call from someone named John. All my family knew it. When the call came, I wasn't home. My daughter Crystal, who was fifteen, answered the phone.

When I got home, I asked, "Were there any calls?'

"Yes," she replied sweetly.

"Well," I asked, "who called?"

"Oh," she said innocently, "somebody named John called."

"John who?" I asked.

"I don't know," she replied, grinning with delight. "I forgot to ask."

Now she knew full well which John had called, but she really enjoyed making me sweat. Ten minutes later John Goff called and said, with real pleasure in his voice, "Sharon, once again, it is my pleasure to congratulate you. Let me be the first to say congratulations to the 1997 National Teacher of the Year!"

I didn't scream this time. I whispered. "Really?" I asked. My face was about to burst from the giant grin on my face.

"Yes, really," he replied. "We are all so proud of you. And by the way, you can't tell anybody!"

Now how was I going to keep such a wonderful thing a secret? My students, my friends, my parents? The White House placed an embargo on the news, which could not be officially announced until April, when the President of the United States greets the new National Teacher of the Year in the Rose Garden. I told my family, and my parents of course, and my principal and superintendent, but the news stayed under wraps until just a couple of days before we left for Washington.

It was a glorious journey, because every step was an unplanned adventure, a new height to climb to and reach. I never planned to reach the summit of that mountain, but the view was spectacular. I knew I had so much to offer the teachers of this country, and others who didn't know or understand the educational world as well. I was proud and ready to begin the next climb, which promised to be a full mountain range, with paths untouched and for which no map was written. But I was ready.

So many confused ideas—where does the rhetoric end

and the true feelings begin? I say to people that I'm proud and humbled and surprised that I was selected as National Teacher of the Year, and I am, but in my heart of hearts, I knew. Through most of the process, I felt confident and relaxed and qualified. One statement that I made to the committee was very true, and I guess I said it with real passion because I really believed it. I have been preparing for this job since I was born, and I didn't even know it. From Mother reading to me and encouraging me through school, to all those days in classes through college, I always liked school. I loved learning, and especially the mental challenge of sucking the information in, assimilating it, storing it, retrieving it, and then sharing it—effectively, and with style.

White House Speech—April 18, 1997

Thank you, Mr. President. Mr. Secretary. Honored guests.

I am so very proud to be a teacher!

I am proud of all of the students whose lives have intersected with mine. And because of that moment in time together, all of us are better. For each of them taught me as well and to them I say, I love you all.

I am proud of my colleagues—three million of us—striving to make a difference in the lives of the children.

This apple, which shines with proud intensity for all teachers, represents

- the knowledge of the past,
- the responsibility of the present,
- and the hope of the future.

As we build this wonderful bridge to the twenty-first century, let us remember that we will need teachers to instruct us how to build it, teachers to guide us across its intricate paths, and teachers who stand ready in the twenty-first century to take us to new paths and bridges as yet undreamed.

And who will walk that path? The children. Imagine a child—any child, every child—hopeful, enthusiastic, curious. In that child sleeps the vision and the wisdom of tomorrow. The touch of a teacher will make the difference.

World Teaching

From Moscow to Ethiopia

I had the opportunity to visit schools in both Russia and Africa. They were vastly different, but reassuringly similar. Moscow was gray and dreary, but the people were wonderful. They were so warm and friendly, and willing to help. They didn't laugh at my atrocious attempts to speak Russian, and they fed me more than I could ever possibly eat! The food was good—very solid, very heavy, and very filling—three times a day! Bottled water was a necessity, unless you wanted champagne, which flowed at every meal, or vodka, which they drink like water. They are very proud people and are fiercely patriotic. "This is RUSSIAN vodka," or "This was painted by a RUSSIAN artist, inspired by a RUSSIAN writer, who went to the very finest RUSSIAN schools."

Similarly, even though Africa was warm and bright orange compared to the cold bleakness of Russia, the people of Africa were just as fiercely patriotic of their countries, boasting of the beauty of Uganda or the friendliness of Togo or the universality of Addis Ababa. The loved their countries and were anxious to show me the distinct and unique qualities that made their country the very best of all.

I had been invited to Moscow by the Russian Teacher of the Year Program to be a part of their selection and celebration of their Teacher of the Year. The philosophy of their program is a bit different than ours. Theirs was more like the Olympics—they pick a "winner" who is designated as the "best" teacher in Russia. I asked them, "Don't you choose your Teacher of the Year to be a representative for all the teachers of Russia? To give honor to teachers everywhere?" They couldn't even comprehend our philosophy.

Their selection process for the finalists is rigorous—much more than any American teacher would do. They must teach two classes of students they have never seen, on a lesson given to them the night before. Twenty judges stand in the room and score the "teaching." Then the finalists must teach again, this time in an auditorium filled with judges and teachers, to a group of people who pretend to be students, on a general topic again assigned the night before. All of this is videotaped under very bright lights. After this presentation, the teacher must stand and answer questions from the judges for thirty minutes to an hour. Most of the questions were really hard—like "How do you teach the history of our country in this math lesson?" or "Why do you teach these students about the problems of pollution? The government has said it is not a problem and you are teaching falsehoods!" One teacher fainted during the "interrogation" process. Several full-time psychologists were on hand to help the teachers with the stress of this selection procedure.

Many of the teachers there had never been away from their provinces before, and for many it was their first trip to Moscow. They were given trips to the Kremlin, the opera, the theater, and the ballet as part of their trip to Moscow, and I was allowed to go with them. There were eighty teachers from across Russia, fifteen semifinalists, five finalists, and one final "winner," who was announced on national television in a two-hour broadcast that included singers, dancers, drummers, and jugglers—a real variety show!

At the end of the ceremony during this TV production, the winning teacher was announced and presented with the "Crystal Pelican" award. (The pelican is the symbol of the teacher in Russia, just as the apple is the symbol for teachers in the United States. The pelican is a bird of nurture, which cares for its young through all odds.) The winning teacher was given a new car, three million rubles (about $500), and a giant pelican made of crystal.

I had an interpreter with me the whole time—an eighteen-year-old student from the University of Moscow who was flighty and forgetful (it was like travelling with my daughter!), but she knew the language and the people and she took good care of me. She spoke English quite well, but she didn't have many opportunities to speak to native speakers, so she was anxious to learn idioms and American curse words! (I'm a teacher—what could I do? I taught her!)

Not surprisingly, the teachers in Russia have the same concerns that we do here. They want their students to succeed, they need more time, and they want more money for what they do. They manage to do so much with so little. A Russian teacher makes about six hundred thousand rubles a month (about $100). In Russian money, we make six million rubles ($1000) in just a few weeks. Yes, the cost of living is lower there, but the cost of goods is still very high. A bar of soap, for example, costs about eighteen thousand rubles ($3). Many of the goods they have are not what we are used to. Toilet paper, for example, is made from recycled newspaper and feels like it—literally! Most of the public bathrooms that I visited did not even bother with toilet paper.

In St. Petersburg I got to visit some schools. I visited a class of fifth graders and, with my interpreter, tried to talk to them in my garbled Russian. A kid in the back raised his hand and said, "Why don't you just speak English?" Then I went to a class of English-speaking juniors and seniors. Their English was flawless and very British. I complimented them on mastering another language, and they said casually, "Oh, English is not our only foreign language. We speak French and German too!" So, in spite of the fact that their school buildings were not very modern, and their methods were also a bit traditional, the results from the classes I visited were phenomenal. There was lots of parental support and an after-school program you would not believe.

About one half of the students in the St. Petersburg schools were enrolled (as their parents and even grandparents had been) in an intensive arts program held in the old palace of Catherine the Great. They had classes in art (eight types to choose from), dancing (ten types to choose from), drama, gymnastics, band (six types to choose from), as well as a Young Cosmonauts Club, a Young Writers Club, a Young Journalists Club, and so on. It was crowded with more than one thousand students, from ages four to nineteen, busy there every day after school and all day Saturday. Many public school teachers taught there (this was not babysitting—this was intense teaching), and many "graduates" of the program returned to teach as well. It was a powerful example of how students who are busy, engaged, and happy have less time to become discipline problems in the streets of the city—any city. These kids went home, did their homework, and fell asleep exhausted. They had no time or energy to become juvenile delinquents. Plus they loved it. It was wonderful.

I was in Africa for an international conference of teachers. Since Africa is made of so many different countries, any conference of teachers there is truly international in scope. Each country has a different cultural base, history, language, monetary system, government, and educational system. In an area that might cover the western part of the United States, one can find dozens of different African countries. It was a large concept to comprehend. A general session, followed by workshops, interrupted by lunch, followed by more workshops—the usual conference agenda, but this one was different. The scope was international, and the message reached far beyond the limited borders of the United States. International schools serve the children of diplomats and businesspeople in those host countries, but they also serve the children of that country, offering them free education, in many cases, with opportunities for advancement impossible in their local schools. Every international school is different, some using a British curriculum, some using an American-based study system, some with hundreds of children from all over the world, and others with just a few children, most of them local residents. How does one teach a class in which the children come from fifty different nationalities, religions, and cultures? And each of those children speaks a different language?

I also got a chance to visit some of the local schools. Eighty to ninety children in a class—sometimes in double shifts—with one teacher. The rooms were bare, with dirt floors and unpainted walls made of cement blocks. No windows, just holes cut in the side for air or rain or wind. The children sat on wooden benches in front of wooden planks for desks. Three, four, even six children crowded together on one bench. They had no supplies, no materials, and one teacher. Yet they were learning, they were extremely well behaved, and they giggled with pleasure at our interruption of their day. They didn't know they were deprived. They had never heard of collaborative learning or multiple intelligences. They only knew school was important and studying was required. So they did. They learned much in spite of extremely difficult circumstances. With one teacher. And no books. And we complain.

The teachers in Africa have the same needs and frustrations as teachers all over the world—they struggle to do their best and are never quite sure if they are reaching that goal. All of them need encouragement and support, whether they are teaching in a gold-mining community, which was so basic they have to make their own soap, or in a school with access to the Internet and an advanced International Baccalaureate program.

As a result of these visits, my eyes were opened to the rest of the world—a world that exists quite well without us, sometimes in spite of us. A world that has no waste because they use everything they have. In Africa they have no plastic bags to throw away their trash because they have no trash. Food is wrapped in banana leaves instead of plastic—who needs plastic? Food is grown, then eaten, then used for fertilizer to begin the process once more. People of two different worlds, Russia and Africa, who know very little of each other, love their countries fiercely, and the parents love their children. Learning takes place under extremely difficult circumstances, and knowledge—admittedly with some difficulty at times—is passed on to the next generation. Much needs to be done to help emerging nations in Africa improve education, because the spark is there. And Russian children who speak several languages have much to teach our children who cannot master even one. We need to help keep that flame lit and realize that we don't have all the answers. Maybe we need to start asking questions instead.

When I boarded the plane to come home from Russia and from Africa, nothing looked better than that sign when I came into the terminal—"Welcome to the United States of America!" I learned many things on those trips—about teachers and learning and the universality of humanity. I'm glad I live here, and I would not want to live there, but we have much to learn from other countries and other cultures.

The Touch of a Teacher

We Make a Difference

Our existence is defined through a series of patterns. Winter's anger is softened by spring, which blooms into the fire of summer. Autumn's glory and despair is forgotten with the wrath of winter once again. Historically and traditionally, the end of the bright freedom of summer marks the beginning of a new school year. Freshly waxed hallways, gleaming with expectation and promise and smelling of chalk dust and challenges, fade into classroom routines and repetitious rhythms. Young minds, like the buds of spring, sprout and bloom with the acquired knowledge of another year, only to return with the fading of the leaves to repeat the cycle once again.

The one constant in this continuum is the teacher, who imparts the wisdom of the past along with the news of the day. Immutable, the teacher guides, instructs, and encourages the continuous and ever-changing mirage of young faces. It is the warmth and wisdom of the teacher that will make a difference in their lives. It is the constancy and consistency of the presence of the teacher around which the educational cycle revolves.

Just as Plato instructed Aristotle, who taught countless others, as educators, the cycle of repeated learning and imparted wisdom is our burden and our joy to continue. The knowledge of the past was given to us, and we, as modern griots, must not only remember the acquired knowledge of past generations but also provide for its perpetuity in the minds of those yet unborn.

Each generation benefits from the knowledge of the past. However, society must grow with the volume of information; no longer will the simple repetition of patterns be sufficient. The body of new information increases exponentially with each succeeding group of learners; therefore, the responsibility of the instructor becomes greater.

Infinite amounts of knowledge exist in the universe, and modern civilization is approaching the capability of touching the edges of enlightenment. Our system of instruction and comprehension must be refined in order to maximize what is able to be imparted to the next generation. Information not yet imagined will influence generations of teachers and learners still to come. Our definitions and interpretation of instruction and education will, of necessity, need to be adjusted, but some realities will remain constant.

For education to occur, there must be a learner, a guider of instruction, and an effective delivery system. This could be accomplished in a traditional classroom with thirty students listening to a teacher in a three-story brick school building. But education also happens in homeless shelters, hospital wards, computer labs, business offices, and parking lots. Education sings in hallways as well as auditoriums, and dances in small rural cottages as well as gleaming city edifices. Education soars when one child and one teacher make the connection between the unknown and the known.

We begin life with a tabula rasa—which is gradually shaded by the colors of our education and experience. It is the teacher who decorates our lives with knowledge. It is a teacher who cheers when the first sentence is mastered, who encourages when long division is difficult, who smiles gently at a first attempt at poetry, and who challenges when a new idea from literature is questioned. Never truly appreciated or acknowledged, the teacher is the silent witness to all our educational accomplishments.

Four hundred years ago someone taught Shakespeare to love the language and to make it sing through the ages. Lincoln, Thoreau, King, Sandburg—all had a teacher who prepared the vision and gave them the courage to fly to its heights. What unknown heroes and artists cower in the darkness, untouched and uninspired? What moment of magic will change their darkness into luminescence?

Magic ceases to exist in a world of reality. Metaphors are lovely, but they fail to cover the harsh reality of overcrowded classrooms, bankrupted budgets, political apathy, and increased social responsibility. Teachers struggle to reach lofty goals, to reach the needs of the students, to merely reach the end of the day. Very little recognition or reward is given for a job on which rests the knowledge of the past, the responsibility of the present, and the hope of the future.

The intrinsic worth of any aspect of modern society is determined through the extrinsic designation of financial value. Sports heroes and entertainment personalities, who provide merely social and recreational release, are willingly and cheerfully paid multimillion-dollar salaries, while teachers, without whom the society would be unable to progress intellectually, are given a pittance and expected to appreciate it. A civilization that honors athletes over intellectuals, that lauds entertainment while denigrating education, and that philosophically separates teachers from the ranks of professionals is a society in danger of destruction.

Teachers, if they are to be what we have asked them to be, must be respected as individuals, scholars, and professionals. They need to be respected as competent in decision making as well as instruction. They should be honored for their accomplishments and rewarded, both professionally and financially, for succeeding in a task that takes skill and dedication and intelligence. Teachers need a support system that is nurturing rather than antagonistic. No longer can teachers be taken for granted as worthless bits of pedagogical insignificance, but rather celebrated for moving civilization from ignorance to enlightenment.

The next century will bring discoveries as yet undreamed. Students must be prepared to become scholars of the universe, and they will need teachers who can provide them with a memory of the past as well as a vision of the future. Those teachers will need to be learners as well, to grow professionally and expand with a world of education that will become increasingly specific and technological. If the best young minds of today are not encouraged to become the educators of tomorrow, who then will teach the children of the twenty-first century? And if a system of financial support, social recognition, and professional development does not exist for those who choose to accept the awesome task of teaching, the educational system will fail, and with it will fail the chances of success for civilization. This might sound like a spurious overstatement, but until education becomes the priority of government, rather than of secondary significance, society will continue to suffer. Education of the populace and recognition of its educators is a matter of cultural and political necessity.

A child, unlike any other, yet identical to all those who have preceded and all who will follow, sits in a classroom today—hopeful, enthusiastic, curious. In that child sleeps the vision and the wisdom of the ages. The touch of a teacher will make the difference.

Books by Sharon M. Draper

* *

From Heinemann   For Teachers of All Ages

Teaching from the Heart
Reflections, Encouragement, and Inspiration

0-325-00131-6

* *

From Simon and Schuster   Ages 12 and up
Tears of a Tiger   0-689-31878-2 (hb)
   Winner, 1995 Coretta Scott King   0-689-80698-1 (pb)
   Genesis Award
Forged by Fire   0-689-80699-X (hb)
   Winner, 1998 Coretta Scott King   0-689-81851-3 (pb)
   Award
Romiette and Julio   0-689-82180-8 (hb)

* *

From Just Us Books   Ages 6–12
The *Ziggy and the Black Dinosaur*™ Series
Ziggy and the Black Dinosaur   0-940-97548-3
Lost in the Tunnel of Time   0-940-97563-7
Shadows of Caesar's Creek   0-940-97576-9

* *

From Scholastic Books   Ages 10–15
JAZZIMAGINATION   0-439-06130-X

* *

From Herwell Press   Poetry Books
Let the Circle Be Unbroken   ISBN: 1-881786-80-3
   Children's poetry
Buttered Bones   ISBN: 1-881786-75-7
   Young adult and adult poetry

* *

From Greenwood Press
"Using *Tears of a Tiger* for Psychological and Literary Analysis"
in **Using Literature to Help Troubled Teenagers Cope
with Family Issues**, ed. Joan Kaywell   ISBN: 0-313-30335-5

* *

You can contact Sharon Draper at *www.sharondraper.com*